The

LIGHT

of the

SUN

CHÖGYAL NAMKHAI NORBU

The LIGHT of the SUN

Teachings on Longchenpa's

PRECIOUS MALA
of THE FOUR DHARMAS

Merigar
58031 Arcidosso (GR)
Italy
www.shangshungpublications.org

Cover image: Oleg Bartunov
Design: Kasia Skura
Transcription: Mae Chen, David Meyer
Editing: Jacob Braverman, Susan Schwarz, Judith Chasnoff
Translation from Tibetan: Jacob Braverman

Commentary based on teachings given at Tashigar Sur, Argentina, from December 27, 2007, to January 3, 2008, and in Moscow, Russia, from May 15 to 19, 2009.

ISBN: 978-88-7834-131-9
IPC — 799EN14 — Approved by the International Publications Committee of the Dzogchen Community founded by Chögyal Namkhai Norbu.

།བློ་ཆོས་སུ་འགྲོ་བར་བྱིན་གྱིས་རློབས།
།ཆོས་ལམ་དུ་འགྲོ་བར་བྱིན་གྱིས་རློབས།
།ལམ་འཁྲུལ་པ་སེལ་བར་བྱིན་གྱིས་རློབས།
།འཁྲུལ་པ་ཡེ་ཤེས་སུ་འཆར་བར་བྱིན་གྱིས་རློབས།

Bless me to turn my mind to the Dharma.
Bless me to take this Dharma as my path.
Bless me to clear away illusion while I am on this path.
Bless me so that illusion itself arises as wisdom.
– Gampopa

Contents

Translator's Preface

THIS BOOK contains the translation of a text composed by the great Dzogchen master Longchen Rabjam Trimed Wözer, commonly known as Longchenpa (1308–1364), together with a commentary by the contemporary Dzogchen master Chögyal Namkhai Norbu. Longchenpa's text is itself based on the famed Four Dharmas of Gampopa (1079-1153), a set of four pith instructions given by that master as a distillation of the entire Buddhist path, which is further condensed into a four-line prayer recited daily by many followers of the Kagyüd tradition. Longchenpa's text, titled *The Precious Mala of the Four Dharmas,* is notable for presenting Gampopa's instructions from the unique perspective of Dzogchen Atiyoga. In 2007 and again in 2009, Chögyal Namkhai Norbu gave detailed oral teachings on Longchenpa's *Precious Mala;* the transcriptions of those teachings have been combined and edited to form the commentary herein.

As Longchenpa describes in his colophon, he wrote *The Precious Mala* spontaneously one night by the light of the moon, as he sat outside his retreat cave in the mountains of central Tibet. This is easy to imagine given the inspired and peaceful tone of his text. It is found within a collection of his works designated as spoken guidance, or *shel-dam,* affirming that it was intended for the ears of students who would take its meaning to heart and apply it directly to their own lives. The directness, detail, and precision of Chögyal Namkhai Norbu's commentary makes it an invaluable key to help us do just that.

This book has benefitted from many people's work. I would like to thank Artur Skura for his patience in guiding the project to completion, Mae Chen and David Meyer for transcribing the oral teachings, Elio Guarisco, Adriano Clemente, and Fabian Sanders for reviewing the translation of the root text and making many improvements, and Judith Chasnoff and Susan Schwarz for final editing.

Any merit arising from the preparation of this book is dedicated to the long life of Chögyal Namkhai Norbu and the flourishing of the Dzogchen transmission in our world.

Jacob Braverman
June 2014

༄། །ཆོས་བཞི་རིན་པོ་ཆེའི་ཕྲེང་བ་ཞེས་བྱ་བ་བཞུགས་སོ། །།

THE PRECIOUS MALA OF THE FOUR DHARMAS

The Light of the Sun

།རྒྱ་གར་སྐད་དུ། །ཙ་ཏུར་དྷརྨ་རཏྣ་སཱ་ལ་ནཱ་མ།
།བོད་སྐད་དུ། །ཆོས་བཞི་རིན་པོ་ཆེའི་ཕྲེང་བ་ཞེས་བྱ་བ།

།སངས་རྒྱས་དང་བྱང་ཆུབ་སེམས་དཔའ་ཐམས་ཅད་ལ་ཕྱག་འཚལ་ལོ།

།གང་གི་རང་བཞིན་ཆོས་སྐུའི་མཁའ་དབྱིངས་ལ།
།ངེས་པ་ལྔ་ལྡན་གཟུགས་སྐུའི་དཀྱིལ་འཁོར་རྒྱས།
།མཛད་པའི་ཟེར་གྱིས་གདུལ་བྱའི་པདྨོ་འཛུམ།
།བདེ་གཤེགས་ཉི་མ་དང་བརྒྱུའི་གཙུག་གིས་མཆོད།

།རྒྱལ་བའི་ཆོས་ཚུལ་རིན་ཆེན་དཔག་བསམ་ཤིང་།
།མ་ལུས་སྲིད་ཞིའི་གདུང་སྐྱོབ་བསིལ་གྲིབ་དེར།
།དད་ལྡན་སྐྱེ་རྒུ་རིམ་གྱིས་འཇུག་པའི་ཚུལ།
།རྣམ་བཞིའི་ཡོན་ཏན་ལྗོན་ཚོགས་བཤད་ཀྱིས་ཉོན།

།གང་ཞིག་མཐའ་མེད་འཁོར་བའི་རྒྱ་མཚོ་ལས།
།བརྒལ་འདོད་རྣམས་ཀྱིས་ཐོག་མར་བསམ་བྱ་བ།
།ཐར་པའི་ཆོས་དེ་ཞི་བདེ་བསྒྲུབ་པའི་ཕྱིར།
།ད་རེས་ཚེ་འདིར་ཡོངས་སུ་འབད་པར་བྱ།

།རྙེད་པར་དཀའ་ཞིང་འཇིག་པར་སླ་བའི་ལུས།
།དལ་འབྱོར་གྲུ་བོ་ཐོབ་དུས་མ་འབད་ན།
།སྲིད་པའི་མཚོ་ལས་ནམ་ཡང་མི་ཐར་ཤིང་།
།སྣ་ཚོགས་སྡུག་བསྔལ་མང་ལྡན་རྒྱུན་མི་འཆད།

།སྐྱེ་ཤིའི་ཆུ་བོ་ཕ་མཐའ་མི་མངོན་ཞིང་།
།ན་རྒའི་ལྦུ་ཕྲེང་ཀུན་ནས་འཁྲུགས་པའི་གནས།
།ཉོན་མོངས་དུས་རླབས་སྲིད་རྩེའི་མཐའ་ཁྱབ་པའི།
།མཚོ་ཆེན་མི་བཟོད་འཇིགས་སུ་རྣམ་པར་རྩེན།

In the language of India, *catur-dharma-ratnamāla-nāma.*
In the language of Tibet, *chö zhi rinpochei trengwa she chawa.*

Homage to all buddhas and bodhisattvas!

Within the *dharmakaya* dimension of space
Unfolds the *rupakaya* mandala endowed with five certainties,
Its rays of activity causing lotus disciples to blossom.
To you who have this nature, sun-like Sugata, I make offerings
with the highest faith.

The teaching of the Conqueror is a precious wish-granting tree,
Giving shelter from the searing heat of samsara and nirvana.
All of you with faith, listen as I explain how to enter, step by step,
Into the refreshing shade of this tree with four precious qualities.

Those who long to go beyond the endless ocean of samsara
First must think, "This time, in this life,
I will truly apply myself to the liberating Dharma
In order to realize peace and happiness."

If you do not strive for this now that you have obtained the ship
Of freedom and advantage – this human body,
so difficult to find and so easily destroyed –
You will never escape the ocean of samsara,
And its stream of sufferings in all their variety will never be cut off.

You will be tossed around in terror on this vast, unbearable sea,
With its endless currents of birth and death,
Its froth of illness and old age converging from all sides,
Its tides of emotion rising to even the peak of existence.

The Light of the Sun

།གང་ཞིག་ཐོས་ནས་སྐྱེ་ཤི་རྒྱུན་ཆད་དེ།
།བདེ་ཆེན་མཆོག་དང་ནམ་ཡང་མི་འབྲལ་བ།
།ཞི་བའི་ཆོས་མཆོག་རིན་ཆེན་གྲུ་བཟང་གིས།
།སྲིད་གསུམ་ཉོན་མོངས་ཆུ་གཏེར་བརྒལ་ཕྱིར་འབད།

།ད་རེས་ཐར་ལམ་བྱང་ཆུབ་མ་བསྒྲུབས་ན།
།ཕྱི་ནས་བདེ་འགྲོའི་མིང་ཡང་མི་གྲགས་ཤིང་།
།ངན་སོང་མཐའ་མེད་གཅིག་ནས་གཅིག་བརྒྱུད་དེ།
།གཏན་དུ་འཁོར་བའི་གནས་ལས་ཐར་ཐབས་མེད།

།དེ་བས་བློ་དང་ལྡན་པའི་སྐྱེ་བོ་རྣམས།
།དལ་དང་འབྱོར་བའི་མི་ལུས་ཐོབ་དུས་འདིར།
།སྙིང་ནས་བརྩོན་པས་ཕན་བདེ་བསྒྲུབ་པར་བྱ།
།དེས་ནི་རང་གཞན་དོན་གཉིས་འགྲུབ་པར་འགྱུར།

།དལ་འབྱོར་ཐོབ་ཀྱང་ཡིད་བརྟན་འགའ་མེད་དེ།
།ཐམས་ཅད་མི་བརྟན་འགྱུར་ཞིང་སྙིང་པོ་མེད།
།སྐད་ཅིག་མི་རྟག་འཇིག་པའི་ཆོས་ཅན་ཏེ།
།མྱུར་དུ་འཆི་ཞེས་སྙིང་ནས་བསམ་པར་བྱ།

།འདི་ལྟར་སྣོད་ཀྱི་འཇིག་རྟེན་ཐམས་ཅད་ཀྱང་།
།མེ་བདུན་ཆུ་གཅིག་རླུང་གིས་འཐོར་བའི་ཚེ།
།སྐྲ་རྩེའི་ལྷག་མ་ཙམ་ཡང་ཡོད་མེད་པར།
།ཐམས་ཅད་སྟོང་སྟེ་ནམ་མཁའ་གཅིག་ཏུ་འགྱུར།

།བཅུད་རྣམས་མི་རྟག་འགྲོ་བ་གཡོ་བ་སྟེ།
།ལྷ་དང་ལྷ་མིན་མི་དང་དུད་འགྲོ་དང་།
།ཡི་དྭགས་དམྱལ་བའི་སེམས་ཅན་ཇི་སྙེད་ཀྱང་།
།དུས་མཐར་འཆི་འཕོ་སྐྱེ་བའི་ཆུ་བོར་བྱིང་།

But whoever, having heard [the Dharma], cuts the stream
of birth and death,
Will never be parted from unsurpassable great bliss.
So strive to cross beyond the sea of the three realms of emotion
On the precious jewel ship, the supreme Dharma of peace.

If you fail to accomplish awakening on the path of liberation this time,
In future lives you will never even hear the names of the joyful realms,
Passing from one state of limitless misery to the next
With no means of ever escaping samsara.

Therefore, those of you with keen intelligence,
Now that you have a human condition of freedom and advantage,
Must strive with all your heart to accomplish benefit and happiness:
This will fulfill both your own aim and that of others.

But even having gained these freedoms and advantages,
there is no security:
Everything is unstable, changeable, without essence,
Momentary, impermanent, subject to destruction.
So think, from deep within your heart, "Soon I will die."

This entire world, the vessel,
Will be emptied and turned to a single space
With not even the tip of a hair remaining
When it is obliterated by seven fires, one flood, and wind.

Its contents, the impermanent beings who move within it –
Devas, asuras, humans, animals, hungry ghosts, and beings of hell:
When their time comes, each one sinks down
Into the waters of death, transmigration, and rebirth.

The Light of the Sun

།ལོ་དང་ཟླ་བ་ཞག་དང་དུས་ཚིགས་དང་།
།སྐད་ཅིག་མི་རྟག་འཇིག་ཅིང་གཡོ་བ་སྟེ།
།དུས་བཞི་འགྱུར་བས་རྣམ་པར་སྐྱོ་བ་ཅན།
།རང་གི་ཚེ་ཡང་མི་རྟག་འགྱུར་བ་སོམས།

།ཡིད་བརྟན་མེད་དོ་ལུས་སྲོག་འབྲལ་དུ་ཉེ།
།སང་དང་བདག་གི་ཚེ་ཟད་དུས་འདི་གཉིས།
།སྔོན་ལ་གང་འབྱུང་ངེས་པ་མེད་དོ་ཞེས།
།དེ་རིང་ཉིད་ནས་ངེས་པར་བསམ་པར་བྱ།

།འཆི་བ་བས་ཀྱང་སྐྱེ་བའི་སྡུག་བསྔལ་འཇིགས།
།གང་དུ་སྐྱེས་ཀྱང་བདེ་བ་འགའ་མེད་དེ།
།འཁོར་བའི་རང་བཞིན་མེ་ཡི་འོབས་ལྟ་བུ།
།འདི་ལས་ད་རེས་ཐར་ཐབས་བཙལ་བར་བྱ།

།དམྱལ་བ་ཚ་གྲང་ཡི་དྭགས་བཀྲེས་དང་སྐོམ།
།དུད་འགྲོ་གཅིག་ཟ་བླེན་རྨོངས་སྡུག་བསྔལ་ཏེ།
།མི་རྣམས་ཉེས་གསུམ་བརྒྱད་ཀྱིས་ཡོངས་སུ་གདུང་།
།ལྷ་མིན་འཐབ་རྩོད་ལྷ་རྣམས་འཆི་འཕོ་ལྟུང་།

།བདེ་སྡུག་འགྱུར་ཞིང་འདུ་བྱེད་སྡུག་བསྔལ་མང་།
།ལྷ་ཡུལ་འབྱོར་བདེ་དག་ལས་ཚེ་འཕོས་ནས།
།སླར་ཡང་དམྱལ་བའི་མེ་ནང་འཇུག་འཚལ་བས།
།འདི་འདྲ་བསམས་ནས་སྲིད་ལས་འདའ་བར་མཛོད།

།ཚེ་འདིའི་སྣང་བ་རྨི་ལམ་སད་ཀ་འདྲ།
།འགྱུར་ཞིང་མི་རྟག་དོར་ནས་འགྲོ་དགོས་པས།
།འཁོར་དང་ལོངས་སྤྱོད་ལ་སོགས་ཅི་ཞིག་བྱ།
།ད་ལྟ་ཉིད་དུ་ཆོས་ལ་འབད་པར་བགྱི།

Years, months, days, hours, and single moments
Are impermanent – they vanish, and [time] moves on.
Because they change, the four seasons have the nature of sorrow and grief.
Consider how your own life is just as impermanent and changing.

So from this moment on, think without fail,
"There is no security! My body and life will soon be parted
And I cannot even know which will come first:
Tomorrow or the end of my life."

The suffering of birth is even more terrifying than death –
There is no joy at all wherever you are born.
By its very nature, samsara is like a pit of flames,
So this time you must seek a way to free yourself from it.

Hell beings are afflicted by heat and cold, *pretas* by hunger and thirst,
Animals by being eaten and by the daze of stupidity.
Humans are tormented by the three faults and eight [conditions],
Asuras by fighting and struggle, *devas* by death and downfall.

Pleasure changes into pain, and myriad sufferings arise
through being conditioned.
Passing away from the celestial realms of abundance, joy, and purity,
We are forced again to enter into the flames of hell.
Reflect on how it really is like this, and leave samsara.

The appearances of this life are like those of a dream just as you are waking:
Shifting and transient, you must leave them behind and go.
Of what use, then, are companions, possessions, and the rest?
From this very moment on, apply yourself to the Dharma.

།འདོད་པ་དུག་དང་མཚོན་དང་མེ་འདྲ་ཞིང་།
།ཡོངས་སུ་གདུངས་བས་བདེ་བའི་གོ་སྐབས་མེད།
།བསགས་དང་བསྲུང་དང་སྤེལ་བས་སྡུག་བསྔལ་ཞིང་།
།ཁེངས་དང་འཇུངས་དང་སེར་སྣས་རྟག་ཏུ་འཆིང་།

།ཀུན་དང་རྩོད་བཅས་ཉོན་མོངས་ཟག་པ་འཕེལ།
།འདུ་འཛིས་གཡེང་ཞིང་ལུས་དང་སྲོག་ལ་རྒོལ།
།དོན་དང་བྱ་བ་མང་ཞིང་ཆོས་དང་འགལ།
།འཕགས་པ་རྣམས་ཀྱིས་རྟག་ཏུ་སྨད་པ་ཡིན།

།འདོད་པ་ཆུང་རྣམས་རང་གིས་དགེ་བ་འཕེལ།
།དེས་ན་ཞི་བའི་ཐར་ལམ་ཞུགས་རྣམས་ཀྱིས།
།འདོད་པ་ཆུང་ཞིང་ཆོག་ཤེས་ལྡན་པར་མཛོད།
།འདོད་པ་ཟད་ན་འཕགས་པ་དངོས་ཡིན་ལ།
།འདོད་པ་ཆུང་ན་འཕགས་པའི་རིགས་ཞེས་བྱ།

།འདོད་ལྡན་སྡུག་བསྔལ་ཉོན་མོངས་འཕེལ་བ་ལྟར།
།འདོད་པ་ཆུང་རྣམས་ངང་གིས་དགེ་བ་འཕེལ།
།དེ་བས་སྔོན་གྱི་དམ་པའི་རྗེས་འགྲོ་བས།
།རྟག་ཏུ་ཆོག་ཤེས་ཡོ་བྱད་བསྟུང་བར་བྱ།

།མི་དང་འགྲོགས་པའི་ཉེས་བའང་ཚད་མེད་དེ།
།དོན་མེད་རྣམ་པར་གཡེངས་ཤིང་བྱ་བའང་མང་།
།ཁྲོ་དང་འཐབ་རྩོད་འཕེལ་ཞིང་ཆགས་སྡང་སྐྱེ།
།རྟག་ཏུ་སྡུག་བསྔལ་འགོ་ཞིང་སྙིང་པོ་མེད།

།ཇི་ལྟར་བྱས་ཀྱང་མགུ་བའི་དུས་མེད་ལ།
།གང་ལྟར་བསྟན་ཀྱང་ཕན་པའི་གོ་སྐབས་དཀའ།
།དེ་ལྟར་མཉན་ཡང་ལེགས་པའི་ཆོས་མེད་ལ།
།བཤེས་ལྟར་མཐུན་ཡང་ཐ་མ་འབྲལ་བར་འགྱུར།

Desire is like a poison, a weapon, or fire:
It overwhelms you with pain, leaving no chance for joy.
Suffering as you amass, protect, and increase,
You are forever shackled by arrogance, possessiveness, and greed.

In conflict with everyone, the emotions that defile you increase;
Caught up in worldly endeavors, you risk your body and life.
With many projects and things to do, you contradict the Dharma
And are always reproached by the Noble Ones.

For those with little desire, virtues naturally increase,
So those who enter the path to the peace of liberation
Should decrease desire and cultivate contentment.
When desire has been extinguished, you are an actual Noble One;
If you have little desire, you are said to be in the family of the Noble Ones.

Just as sufferings and emotions grow for those who have desire,
For those with little desire, virtues spontaneously increase.
So to follow in the footsteps of the holy beings of the past,
Be content at all times and reduce your possessions.

Keeping close ties with others brings inestimable harm:
You are totally and meaninglessly distracted, and have many things to do;
Hostilities and strife proliferate, attachment and hatred emerge.
You are constantly infected by these sufferings, and this is pointless.

Whatever you have done, they will never be satisfied.
However you try to teach them, the chances of benefit are slim.
Even when they do listen, they lack the excellent qualities [to understand].
And however harmoniously you relate to them,
you will separate in the end.

The Light of the Sun

།དེ་བས་འཁོར་དང་མཛའ་བཤེས་གཉེན་འདུན་ལ།
།ཉེ་བར་བརྟེན་པའི་འབྲེལ་འདྲིས་ཀུན་སྤང་ཏེ།
།གཅིག་པུར་དབེན་པར་དམ་ཆོས་སྒྲུབ་པའི་ཕྱིར།
།དེ་རིང་ཉིད་ནས་ངེས་པར་འབད་པར་བྱ།

།སྔོན་གྱི་སྐྱེ་བོ་དམ་པ་མཆོག་རྣམས་ཀྱང་།
།དབེན་པར་གནས་ལས་བདུད་རྩི་བརྙེས་ཞེས་གསུངས།
།དེ་ཕྱིར་བདག་ཀྱང་ཞི་བ་སྒྲུབ་པའི་ཕྱིར།
།ནགས་ནང་དབེན་པ་གཅིག་པུར་གནས་པར་བྱ།

།དབེན་པའི་གནས་ནི་རྒྱལ་བ་རྣམས་ཀྱིས་བསྔགས།
།མི་སྤུན་མི་མེད་ཟབ་མོའི་ཏིང་འཛིན་འཕེལ།
།ངང་གིས་ཆོས་འགྲུབ་མི་རྟག་སྐྱོ་ཤེས་སྐྱེ།
།ཡོ་བྱད་སྤུངས་ཤིང་འདུ་འཛི་རྣམ་གཡེང་མེད།
།དད་དང་ངེས་འབྱུང་ཡོན་ཏན་ཚོགས་མང་ཞིང་།
།འབྲེལ་འདྲིས་མེད་པས་ངང་གིས་བྱ་བ་ཉུང་།

།གཞན་གྱི་སེམས་འཛིན་ངོ་སྲུང་ཆོས་བརྒྱད་མེད།
།རང་དབང་འགྱུར་བདེ་ཉེན་མཚན་ཆོས་ཀྱིས་འདའ
།།དལ་འབྱོར་དོན་ཡོད་སྒྲུབ་པ་སྙིང་པོར་བྱེད།
།དེ་སོགས་ཡོན་ཏན་བརྗོད་ཀྱིས་མི་ལང་བས།
།གཅིག་པུར་རབ་ཏུ་དབེན་པའི་ནགས་ཁྲོད་དུ།
།ཚེ་གང་ཟབ་མོའི་ཏིང་འཛིན་བསྒྲུབ་པར་བྱ།

So abandon all relationships of mutual dependence
With followers, close friends, and family,
And from this day forward sincerely strive
To accomplish the sacred Dharma in solitude.

The supreme holy beings of the past have said
They found the nectar [of realization] by abiding in solitude.
So I too will remain alone in the solitude of the forest
In order to accomplish the state of peace.

Places of solitude are praised by the conquerors:
Far from rough people, profound contemplation flourishes,
The Dharma is accomplished naturally, and disillusionment
arises toward impermanent phenomena.
You cast off your possessions and remain
without the diversion of worldly endeavors.
You amass abundant good qualities of faith and renunciation,
And without ties to others your tasks naturally become few.

With no need to please others or to save face,
and free from the eight worldly concerns,
You have the fortune and joy of independence,
and pass day and night in the practice of Dharma.
You give meaning to your condition of freedom and advantage
by applying the essence of the practice.
These and other qualities of solitude exceed description,
So remain alone in the perfect solitude of the forest
Practicing profound contemplation for the rest of your life.

The Light of the Sun

།དེ་ལྟར་ལེགས་གསུང་ཆོས་ཀྱི་ཆར་བསིལ་བས།
།ཉོན་མོངས་གདུང་བའི་རྟོག་པ་རབ་ཞི་ནས།
།ཏིང་འཛིན་དགེ་ཚོགས་པད་མཚོ་རབ་གང་སྟེ།
།ཞི་བའི་གནས་ན་འབྱོར་པ་རབ་རྒྱས་ཤོག

།ཆོས་བཞི་རིན་པོ་ཆེའི་ཕྲེང་བ་ལས།
།བློ་ཆོས་སུ་འགྲོ་བའི་རབས་ཏེ་དང་པོའོ།

།དེ་ལྟར་རབ་དཀར་དམ་པའི་ཆོས་མཆོག་ལ།
།དད་པས་རབ་ཞུགས་ཐར་ལམ་འདོད་རྣམས་ཀྱིས།
།རང་གི་སེམས་ཉིད་རབ་ཏུ་གདུལ་བྱའི་ཕྱིར།
།ཆོས་དེ་ལམ་དུ་འགྲོ་བ་རབ་ཏུ་གཅེས།

།འདི་ལྟར་རྒྱལ་བའི་བསྟན་ལ་རབ་ཞུགས་ནས།
།ཐོས་བསམ་སྒོམ་པར་ཆས་པ་དེ་དག་ཀྱང་།
།ཁ་ཅིག་མ་ཞི་རང་རྒྱུད་ངན་པ་དང་།
།ལ་ལ་ལམ་ལོག་དམན་དང་ལམ་གོལ་ཞུགས།

།འདོད་སྲེད་ཆེ་དང་ཚེ་འདིར་གཡེངས་ལ་སོགས།
།ཆོས་དང་འགལ་བའི་ཉེས་པ་དེ་དག་ཀུན།
།ཆོས་དེ་ལམ་དུ་མ་སོང་དག་ལས་བྱུང་།

།དེ་ལས་འདི་ཕྱིའི་ཉེས་པ་ཚད་མེད་དེ།
།འཁྲུལ་པས་བསླུས་གང་འཆི་ཁར་འགྱོད་པ་ཉིད།
།བར་དོར་འཇིགས་དངངས་ཕྱི་མར་ངན་སོང་འགྲོ།
།གཏན་དུ་སྲིད་ལས་ཐར་པའི་སྐབས་མེད་དོ།
།དེ་བས་ཆོས་དེ་ལམ་དུ་འགྲོ་བར་བྱ།

May this cooling rain of well-spoken Dharma
Completely pacify the thoughts that burn you in the heat of emotions;
May it fill the lotus lake of the gathering of contemplation and virtue,
And in this place of peace, may fortune reach full blossom.

From *The Precious Mala of the Four Dharmas,* this is the first teaching, on turning your mind to the Dharma.

Having entered, through faith, into this pure, sacred, and supreme Dharma,
It is most crucial for those of you who long [to travel]
the path to liberation,
To take this Dharma as a path
In order to thoroughly tame your minds.

Even among those who have entered the teachings of the conquerors
And have begun to listen, reflect, and meditate upon them,
Some remain restless, in negative states of mind,
While others stray onto perverse, inferior, or mistaken paths.

Being strongly conditioned by cravings and desires,
preoccupied with the concerns of this life,
And all other such faults that contradict the Dharma
Arise from your not having applied this Dharma as a path.

This leads to problems beyond measure, both in this life and the next.
Those who are deceived by illusions
have only regret at the moment of death,
Terror and panic in the intermediate state,
and rebirth in the realms of misery:
They never have the chance to free themselves from samsara.
This is why you must apply the Dharma as a path.

The Light of the Sun

།ཇི་ལྟར་ནད་ཀྱི་གཉེན་པོར་མི་དག་གིས།
།བཀྲུ་སྨན་སྦྱར་ཡང་དེ་ཉིད་མ་དག་ན།
།ཡོངས་སུ་གདུང་བས་སྨར་ལ་གདུངས་པ་བཞིན།
།གཉེན་པོར་མ་སོང་ཆོས་ལ་དགོས་པ་ཅི།
།འདི་ན་དེ་འདྲའི་ཉེས་པ་ཚད་མེད་པས།
།དད་ལྡན་སྐྱེ་བོས་ལེགས་པར་ཤེས་པར་བྱ།

།དེ་ལ་ཆོས་དེ་ལམ་དུ་འགྲོ་བ་ནི།
།ཐོག་མར་དགེ་བའི་བཤེས་ལ་རག་ལས་པས།
།མཚན་ལྡན་བླ་མ་དམ་པ་བསྟེན་པ་གཅེས།
།དེ་ལས་ལེགས་རྒྱུའི་ཡོན་ཏན་དུ་མ་འབྱུང་།

།དེ་ཡང་ཐབས་མཁས་ཐུགས་རྗེའི་བདག་ཉིད་ཅན།
།ཞི་ཞིང་དུལ་བ་བཟོད་དང་ལྡན་པ་སྟེ།
།སྡོམ་དང་དམ་ཚིག་སྤྱོད་ཚུལ་ཕུན་སུམ་ཚོགས།
།མང་དུ་ཐོས་ཤིང་ལེགས་པར་སྦྱངས་པ་ཆེ།
།བྱིན་རླབས་ཚད་མེད་གཞན་སྣང་རང་གིས་འགྱུར།
།ཚེ་འདི་མ་འདྲེས་ཆོས་བརྒྱུད་མཁའ་ལྟར་དག

།འབྲེལ་ཚད་དོན་ལྡན་ཐར་ལམ་འགོད་པ་འདི།
།སྙིགས་མའི་དུས་སུ་རྒྱལ་བའི་རྣམ་འཕྲུལ་ཏེ།
།རབ་དང་གུས་པ་ཆེན་པོས་བསྟེན་པར་བྱ།

If the remedy for an illness is used incorrectly,
Though applied as a salve it is toxic instead,
Causing great pain that only prolongs your torment.
Likewise, what use is the Dharma if it does not serve
as a remedy?
If misapplied, it will cause immeasurable harm,
So those with faith must understand this well.

Applying the Dharma as a path depends, before all else,
On having a teacher of virtue.
So it is crucial to rely upon a sublime qualified master,
The source of myriad excellent qualities.

Such a master is adept in skillful methods,
and is the very embodiment of compassion.
He is calm, disciplined, and patient.
His way of applying the vows and *samayas* is perfect
and complete.
His learning is vast, his training excellent and thorough.
His immeasurable blessings naturally transform
the vision of others.
He is not entangled in the affairs of this life,
and is as pure of the eight worldly dharmas as space itself.

Any connection made with him is meaningful
and establishes you on the path to liberation.
Such a master is a manifestation of the Conqueror in these
degenerate times,
So rely on him with a pure mind and the highest respect.

The Light of the Sun

།དེ་ལས་ཕན་ཡོན་ཚད་མེད་ཟད་མེད་དེ།
།སྲིད་ལ་སྐྱོ་ཞིང་ངེས་འབྱུང་བློ་སྣ་ཐུང་།
།ཚེ་འདི་བློས་ཐོངས་འཁྲུལ་སྣང་བདག་འཛིན་འཛིག
།ངང་གིས་དུལ་ཞིང་ཐོས་བསམ་སྒོམ་པ་ལྡན།
།དད་སོགས་རྒྱ་ཆེ་སྦྱངས་བའི་ཡོན་ཏན་ལྡན།
།ཚེ་འདི་དོན་ཡོད་ཕྱི་མ་འབྲས་དང་བཅས།
།དེ་ཕྱིར་དམ་པ་རྣམས་ལ་བསྟེན་པར་བྱ།

།དེ་ཡང་རང་གི་སྒོ་གསུམ་ཟོལ་མེད་པས།
།ནད་པས་སྨན་པ་ཚོང་པས་དེད་དཔོན་དང་།
།གྲུ་པས་མཉན་པ་མགྲོན་པོས་སྐྱེལ་མ་ལྟར།
།གུས་པའི་སྲི་ཞུས་རྟག་ཏུ་མཉེས་པར་བྱ།

།མ་དད་ལོག་པར་ལྟ་བའི་སེམས་སྐྱེས་ན།
།སྐད་ཅིག་གྲངས་བཞིན་ངན་འགྲོར་འཇུག་པར་གསུངས།
།དེ་བས་བཤགས་སྡོམ་འགྱོད་ཚངས་ཆེན་པོ་ཡིས།
།དམ་ཚིག་རྣམ་དག་མིག་བཞིན་བསྲུང་ལ་འབད།

།དེ་ལྟར་བཤེས་གཉེན་དམ་པ་རབ་བསྟེན་ནས།
།ཐོས་བསམ་སྒོམ་པས་རང་རྒྱུད་སྦྱངས་བྱས་ནས།
།ཐར་པ་ཁོ་ན་འདོད་པའི་བསམ་པ་ཡིས།
།གང་བྱེད་དགེ་བ་འདུན་པས་བསྒྱུར་བ་ནི།
།ཆོས་དེ་ལམ་དུ་འགྲོ་བའི་མན་ངག་ཡིན།

The benefits of doing so are immeasurable and inexhaustible:
Disillusioned with samsara, you renounce it and curtail your plans;
You cast away thoughts of this present life,
    and your clinging to the reality of illusory vision collapses;
You become naturally disciplined, and are endowed with
    listening, reflection, and meditation.
Possessing faith and myriad other qualities of training,
Your present life becomes truly meaningful,
    and in future lives you will experience the fruits of this.
This is why you should rely on sublime masters.

In this regard, without deception or artifice in your three gates,
Be like a patient with his doctor, a merchant with his captain,
A passenger with his ferryman, and a traveler with his guide,
And always please your master with respectful and devoted service.

It is said that you will enter the lower realms
As many times as the number of moments
    for which you hold a faithless, perverse view of your teacher.
So guard the purity of your *samayas* as you would your own eyes
By confessing [faults] with great remorse
    and vowing [to not repeat them].

Having come to rely in this way upon a sublime teacher of virtue,
And having trained your mind through listening, reflection,
    and meditation,
Transform everything you do into the pursuit of virtue
By thinking only of the desire for liberation.
This is the quintessential instruction
    for applying the Dharma as a path.

The Light of the Sun

།ཉན་དང་སེམས་དང་ཁ་ཧྭན་བྱེད་པ་ནའང་།
།རང་རྒྱུད་ཐར་པའི་དོན་དུ་དེ་བརྩམ་ཞིང་།
།འབྲི་དང་གློག་དང་འཛིན་དང་འཆད་པ་ནའང་།
།ཐར་པ་ཕོ་ན་འདོད་པས་བརྩམ་པར་བྱ།

།སྒོམ་དང་ལྟ་དང་སྤྱོད་པར་བྱེད་པ་ནའང་།
།ཐར་པ་ཕོ་ནའི་སེམས་དང་མ་བྲལ་བས།
།ངེས་འབྱུང་སྐྱོ་ཤས་དྲག་པོས་འབད་པར་བྱ།
།སྙིང་པོའི་མན་ངག་འདི་ལས་གོང་ན་མེད།

།ཟ་ཉལ་འགྲོ་འདུག་སྨྲ་བརྗོད་བསམ་ལ་སོགས།
།མདོར་ན་བྱ་བ་གང་དང་གང་བྱེད་ཀྱང་།
།ཐར་པ་འདོད་པའི་བློ་དང་མ་བྲལ་བས།
།སྐྱོ་ཤས་བསྐྱེད་དེ་སེམས་རྒྱུད་གདུལ་བར་བྱ།
།འདི་ནི་དམ་ཆོས་ལམ་དུ་འགྲོ་བའི་གནད།

།ཁྱད་པར་ཐེག་ཆེན་ལམ་དུ་འགྲོ་བྱེད་པ།
།དགེ་བ་གང་བྱེད་གཞན་དོན་དམིགས་པ་སྟེ།
།སྙིང་རྗེས་སེམས་བསྐྱེད་སྨོས་བསྔོ་ཡི་རང་ཞིང་།
།སེམས་ཅན་དོན་ཕྱིར་ཡོངས་སུ་བསྔབ་པའོ།

།འདི་ལྟར་འགྲོ་ཀུན་བདག་གི་ཕ་དང་མ།
།གཉེན་དང་རྩ་ལག་ཕན་གདགས་ཞིང་ཡིན་ལ།
།བདག་ཀྱང་གཞན་དོན་བྱང་ཆུབ་སེམས་བསྐྱེད་པས།
།འགྲོ་བའི་དོན་དུ་དགེ་བ་བསྒྲུབ་པར་བྱ།
།བདག་གི་དགེ་བས་འགྲོ་བ་བདེ་བར་འགྱུར།

When you listen to teachings, reflect on them,
 or recite them aloud,
Do so for the sake of liberating your mind.
When you write, read, memorize, or explain,
Do so only out of desire for liberation.

When you apply the meditation, view, and conduct,
Strive with intense disillusionment and renunciation
By never separating from this single-minded focus upon liberation.
There is nothing higher than this,
 the heart of quintessential instructions.

When you eat, sleep, walk, sit, speak, think –
In short, in each and every thing you do –
Arouse disillusionment [toward samsara] and tame your mind
By never being without the desire for liberation.
This is the vital point for applying the sacred Dharma as a path.

In particular, to take the Mahayana Dharma as your path,
Every act of virtue is done with the benefit of others in mind.
Through compassion, you arouse *bodhichitta,*
 make aspirations and dedications, and rejoice,
And strive wholeheartedly to accomplish the benefit of beings.

"All these beings have been my own father and mother,
The friends and family I have wanted to help.
So by arousing the *bodhichitta* that benefits others,
I must accomplish virtue for their sake.
May my virtue bring these beings to happiness!"

The Light of the Sun

།དེ་ཀུན་སྡུག་བསྔལ་བདག་ལ་སྨིན་པ་དང་།
།བདག་གི་དགེ་བ་འགྲོ་ལ་སྨིན་གྱུར་ཏེ།
།ལུས་ཅན་ཐམས་ཅད་སངས་རྒྱས་ཐོབ་པར་ཤོག
།སྙམ་དུ་ཚད་མེད་སྙིང་རྗེའི་སེམས་བསྐྱེད་སྦྱངས།

།དགེ་བ་གང་རྣམས་སྦྱོར་བ་སེམས་བསྐྱེད་དང་།
།དངོས་གཞི་མི་དམིགས་རྗེས་ལ་བསྔོ་བ་བྱ།

།དེ་ཡང་འཁོར་གསུམ་ཡོངས་སུ་དག་པ་ནི།
།སྦྱང་བྱ་སྦྱོང་བྱེད་ཡོངས་སུ་སྦྱང་བ་པོ།
།སྒྱུ་འདྲ་མེད་ལ་སྣང་ཙམ་སྤྲུལ་པ་བཞིན།
།རང་བཞིན་དག་པས་གཞན་གྱི་དོན་ཕྱིར་བསྔོ།

།སོས་པ་རྒྱལ་དང་རྒྱལ་བའི་ཆོས་རྣམས་དང་།
།རྒྱལ་སྲས་དམ་པ་རྣམས་དང་བསོད་ནམས་ཞིང་།
།མ་ལུས་ཀུན་ལ་རབ་ཏུ་དད་པ་སྐྱེ།
།རང་དོན་གཉིས་དོན་གཞན་དོན་སོས་པ་ལས།
།བསྟོད་དང་བཀུར་དང་བསྔགས་པ་དཔེ་མེད་ཐོབ།

།ཡི་རང་རྒྱལ་དང་དེ་སྲས་འགྲོ་ཀུན་དང་།
།དགེ་བ་ཀུན་ལ་དགའ་བ་སྒོམ་པ་སྐྱེ།
།འདི་ནི་བསོད་ནམས་ཕུང་པོ་དཔག་ཏུ་མེད།
།ཚད་མེད་ཆེན་པོར་བསྒྱུར་བའི་ཐབས་མཆོག་ཡིན།
།སྨོན་ལམ་རྣམ་དག་འགྲོ་བའི་དོན་ཕྱིར་གདབ།
།སྤྱོད་ཡུལ་དག་པའི་མན་ངག་བསྒོམ་པར་བྱ།

"May all their sufferings ripen in me.
May my virtues ripen in them.
And may all embodied beings attain buddhahood!"
Thinking this, train in arousing immeasurably
compassionate *bodhichitta.*

Whatever virtue you perform, begin by arousing *bodhichitta,*
Perform the act itself without conceptual fixation,
and conclude by dedicating the merit.

The utterly pure three spheres –
The object of training, the act of training,
and the one who wholeheartedly applies this training –
Are nonexistent, like illusions; they are mere appearances, like forms
conjured by magic.
By means of this natural purity, dedicate your merit to the benefit of others.

Aspiration means that, with total faith in all fields of merit –
The conquerors, their teachings, and their sublime children –
You aspire to your own benefit, the twofold benefit,
and the benefit of others.
From this you gain praise, honor, and veneration beyond compare.

Rejoicing means cultivating joy toward every virtue
Of the conquerors, their children, and all beings.
It is the supreme method that transforms
Boundless heaps of merit into a great infinitude.
Make prayers of total purity to fulfill the purpose of others;
Apply the essential instructions on the purity of the field
of perception.

The Light of the Sun

།ཐ་མལ་ཕྱོགས་སུ་སྐད་ཅིག་མ་ཡེངས་པར།
།སྒོ་གསུམ་དགེ་བ་གཞན་དོན་སྙིང་པོར་བྱ།
།རང་རྒྱུད་བདུལ་ནས་ལྷག་པའི་སེམས་བསྐྱེད་ལྡན།
།ཆོས་གང་ལམ་དུ་འགྲོ་ཞེས་བྱ་བ་ལགས།

།དེ་ལྟར་དོན་ཟབ་ངོ་མཚར་ཛ་སྦྲའི་དབྱངས།
།ཟབ་ཅིང་རྒྱ་ཆེའི་ང་རོ་སྙན་གྲགས་པ།
།མ་རིག་གཉིད་མྱོས་འགྲོ་ཀུན་རབ་སད་དེ།
།ཞི་བའི་དགའ་སྟོན་རྒྱ་ཆེར་མཐོང་བར་ཤོག

།ཆོས་བཞི་རིན་པོ་ཆེའི་ཕྲེང་བ་ལས།
།ཆོས་ལམ་དུ་འགྲོ་བའི་རབས་ཏེ་གཉིས་པའོ།

།དེ་ནས་ལམ་གྱི་འཁྲུལ་པ་སེལ་བ་ཡང་།
།ཐུན་མོང་ཁྱད་པར་བླ་ན་མེད་པ་ལས།

།དང་པོ་ཐུན་མོང་ཐེག་པའི་ལམ་ཆེན་གང་།
།ཚད་མེད་སེམས་བསྐྱེད་སྨོན་ལམ་སྙིང་རྗེའི་བདག
།ཐབས་ཆེན་སྤྱོད་པས་འཁྲུལ་པ་སེལ་བ་སྟེ།
།སྟོང་ཉིད་སྙིང་རྗེའི་སྙིང་པོ་དང་ལྡན་ཞིང་།
།རང་གཞན་དོན་གཉིས་ཀུན་ཏུ་སྒྲུབ་པ་ན།

Without becoming distracted by ordinary concerns
for even a single moment,
Practice virtue with your three gates as the essence
of benefit for others.
Having tamed your own mind, imbue it with
the extraordinary intention [of *bodhichitta*]:
This is what is meant by making whatever Dharma [you apply]
into a path.

May the music of this wondrous drum
of the profound meaning,
With its eminent roar, profound and vast,
Fully awaken all beings from the drunken sleep
of ignorance
To behold the vast festival of peace.

From *The Precious Mala of the Four Dharmas,* this is the second teaching,
on applying the Dharma as a path.

Then, there are common, special, and unsurpassed ways
To clear away illusion on the path.

First, on the general path of the Mahayana,
As a practitioner of immeasurable *bodhichitta,*
aspiration prayers, and compassion,
You clear away illusion by means of extraordinary conduct:
When you are endowed with the essence
of emptiness and compassion
And work continuously to accomplish the twofold benefit
of self and other,

།ཆོས་ཁམས་དགེ་བ་འདུས་མ་བྱས་པ་ཡི།
།གློ་བུར་དྲི་མ་རབ་ཏུ་སྦྱངས་པའི་ཕྱིར།
།ཚོགས་དང་སྦྱོར་མཐོང་སྒོམ་པའི་ལམ་བཞི་རུ།
།བྱང་ཆུབ་ཕྱོགས་ཆོས་སུམ་ཅུ་བདུན་བསྒོམ་ཞིང་།
།དག་པའི་ལྟ་བ་སྟོང་ཉིད་བཅུ་དྲུག་དང་།
།སྨོན་མེད་སྤྱོད་པ་ཕ་རོལ་ཕྱིན་དྲུག་རྫོགས།

།གང་ཟག་ཆོས་བདག་གཉིས་པོ་མེད་རྟོགས་ནས།
།ཉོན་མོངས་གཉེན་པོའི་ཐབས་ཀྱིས་སྦྱོང་བ་ནི།
།བྱང་ཆུབ་སེམས་དཔའ་རྣམས་ཀྱི་ལམ་བཟང་སྟེ།
།སྒྱུ་མ་རྨི་ལམ་འཁྲུལ་པའི་ཚུལ་ཙམ་ལས།
།སྤང་བླང་དོན་བྱས་དགེ་སྡིག་བླང་དོར་བྱེད།
།འདོད་ཆགས་ཞེ་སྡང་གཏི་མུག་ཉོན་མོངས་ལ།
།མི་གཙང་བྱམས་དང་རྟེན་འབྲེལ་ཆུ་བོས་སྦྱོང་།

།དམ་པའི་དོན་དུ་མ་སྐྱེས་རྣམ་དག་པས།
།འཁོར་འདས་གཉིས་མེད་སྤྲོས་དང་བྲལ་བ་སྟེ།
།བདེན་པ་གཉིས་དོན་རྟེན་ཅིང་འབྲེལ་འབྱུང་ལམ།
།མཚན་ཉིད་རྒྱུ་ཡི་ཐེག་པ་ཆེན་པོ་ལགས།

For the sake of utterly cleansing the temporary stains
From the virtuous and unconditioned nature of phenomena,
You cultivate the thirty-seven factors of awakening
As you traverse the paths of accumulation, application,
seeing, and meditation,
Perfecting the authentic view of the sixteen emptinesses
And the faultless conduct of the six *paramitas.*

Having realized that there is no self in either beings
or phenomena,
To then train in methods that remedy the emotions
Is the excellent path of the bodhisattvas.
Though things exist in no more than the illusory manner
of a dream or a magical display,
You give meaning to rejecting and accepting
by taking up virtue and casting off vice,
And wash away the emotions of attachment, anger,
and ignorance
With the water of [meditation on] impurity, love,
and interdependence.

Within absolute truth, samsara and nirvana
are unborn and totally pure,
So they are nondual and free from conceptual elaboration.
This path on which the meaning of the two truths arises
in interdependence
Is the causal Mahayana vehicle of characteristics.

The Light of the Sun

།ཁྱད་པར་ལམ་ཆེན་གསང་སྔགས་ཕྱི་ནང་སྟེ།
།བསྐྱེད་རྫོགས་ཟུང་འཇུག་ཐབས་མཆོག་དཔག་ཏུ་མེད།
།སྣ་ཚོགས་རིམ་པས་འཕྲུལ་པ་སྦྱོང་བ་སྟེ།

།གསང་སྔགས་ཕྱི་གསུམ་དག་པ་གཙོར་བྱེད་པས།
།སྤང་བླང་རིས་འཛོག་དྲི་མ་གཉེན་པོས་སེལ།
།ནང་ནི་ཟུང་འཇུག་གཉིས་མེད་ཡེ་ཤེས་ཀྱིས།
།སྤང་བྱའི་དངོས་དེ་ཐབས་ཀྱིས་ལམ་དུ་བསྒྱུར།

།བདེ་གཤེགས་སྙིང་པོའི་གཞི་དབྱིངས་དཀྱིལ་འཁོར་ལ།
།རང་སྣང་ཆོས་ཀུན་རང་སེམས་སྣང་བ་ཙམ།
།འཕྲུལ་པ་དངོས་མེད་སྟོང་གཟུགས་གསལ་སྣང་ཉིད།
།ཕུང་པོ་ཁམས་དང་སྐྱེ་མཆེད་ལ་སོགས་པ།
།རིགས་ལྔ་ལ་སོགས་དག་པར་དྲན་བྱས་ཏེ།
།བསྐྱེད་པའི་རིམ་པས་སྣང་སྲིད་དཀྱིལ་འཁོར་གཅིག
།ལུས་ལྷ་ངག་སྔགས་དྲན་རྟོག་འགྲོ་འདུར་སྦྱོང་།
།ཐ་མར་འཕྲུལ་སྣང་སངས་རྒྱས་ཞིང་དུ་བལྟ།

།རྫོགས་པའི་རིམ་པས་ཐམས་ཅད་ཆོས་ཉིད་དང་།
།བསམ་གྱིས་མི་ཁྱབ་འོད་གསལ་དབྱིངས་ལ་འཇུག
།རྩ་དང་རླུང་དང་ཐིག་ལེའི་རྣལ་འབྱོར་གྱིས།
།རླུང་སེམས་ལས་རུང་དབྱིངས་དང་ཡེ་ཤེས་སྦྱོར།

On the special, great path of the outer and inner Secret Mantra
You purify illusion in various stages
Through innumerable supreme methods
of development, completion, and their union.

On the three outer levels of Secret Mantra,
by mainly emphasizing purity,
You alternate between rejecting and accepting
as antidotes to clear away defilements.
On the inner levels, by means of the wisdom of nondual union,
The very things that were to be abandoned
are transformed through skillful methods into the path itself.

In the *sugatagarbha* mandala of the real condition of the base,
All self-manifest phenomena are merely the display of your own mind:
They are illusory and without substance,
luminous appearances of empty form.
Having engendered the recollection of the purity of the aggregates,
elements, sense faculties, and so forth
As being the five buddha families and so forth,
By means of the development stage, the entire scope of phenomena
arises as one mandala.
Your body is purified into deity, your speech into mantra, and
thought activity into the emanation and reabsorption [of wisdom],
Until finally illusory vision is perceived as the buddhafield.

By means of the completion stage, everything enters into the dimension
Of the real nature and inconceivable luminous clarity.
Through the yogas of the channels, energies, and essences,
Your energies and mind acquire special pliancy,
and the real condition and wisdom are unified.

The Light of the Sun

།བྱང་འཇུག་དབྱེར་མེད་ཕྱག་རྒྱ་ཆེན་པོའི་ལམ།
།འབྲས་བུ་གསང་སྔགས་རྡོ་རྗེ་ཐེག་པ་ལགས།

།བླ་མེད་ཐེག་པ་མཆོག་གསང་རྫོགས་པ་ཆེ།
།ལྷུན་གྲུབ་དབྱིངས་ལ་དངོས་སུ་སྦྱོར་བ་སྟེ།

།གཞི་དབྱིངས་མི་འགྱུར་ནམ་མཁའ་ལྟ་བུ་ལ།
།ཡོན་ཏན་ལྷུན་གྲུབ་ཉི་ཟླ་གཟའ་སྐར་བཞིན།
།བཙལ་བ་མེད་པར་ཡེ་ནས་ལྷུན་གྲུབ་པས།
།འབད་ཅིང་རྩོལ་མེད་རང་བཞིན་མངོན་སུམ་ལམ།

།འོད་གསལ་དབྱིངས་ཀྱི་དཀྱིལ་འཁོར་འདུས་མ་བྱས།
།རང་གནས་ཆོས་སྐུ་མཉམ་པའི་དགོངས་པ་ཉིད།
།རྫོགས་པར་བྱེད་པ་གནས་ལུགས་ལྟ་བའི་མཆོག

།དག་པའི་དབྱིངས་ལ་གློ་བུར་སྒྲིབ་པའི་སྤྲིན།
།འགྲོ་སེམས་འཁྲུལ་སྣང་མེད་བཞིན་སྣང་བ་ཡིས།
།ཁམས་གསུམ་རིགས་དྲུག་བརྒྱུད་ཅིང་ཅིར་སྣང་ཡང་།
།སྣང་བའི་དུས་ན་དོན་ལ་གྲུབ་པ་མེད།
།མཁའ་དང་སྤྲིན་བཞིན་གློ་བུར་རྐྱེན་སྣང་ཙམ།

This is the path of the indivisible union of Mahamudra,
The fruitional Secret Mantra Vajra Vehicle.

In the unexcelled vehicle of the supreme and secret
Total Perfection,
You connect directly with your self-perfected real condition.

In the real condition of the base, like the changeless sky,
All qualities are self-perfected, like the sun, moon, and stars.
And since they are self-perfected in this way from the beginning,
with no need to be sought,
This is the path on which your real nature manifests directly,
without effort or exertion.

The supreme view of the natural state brings you to the realization
Of the state of equality of naturally abiding *dharmakaya*,
The uncompounded mandala of the real condition
of luminous clarity.

In the expanse of purity of the real condition,
A passing veil of clouds – the illusory display of beings' minds –
Appears without existing and causes them to traverse the three realms
and six classes.
But however these phenomena manifest, they have no reality,
even in their moment of appearing:
Like clouds in the sky, they are just a display
of passing conditions.

།འཁོར་བ་སྒྲོ་བཏགས་མཚན་ཉིད་ཆད་པ་སྟེ།
།མེད་བཞིན་སྣང་སྟེ་རང་གི་ངོ་བོས་སྟོང་།
།སྟོང་སྣང་དངོས་མེད་རབ་རིབ་སྐྲ་ཤད་དང་།
།རྨི་ལམ་སྒྱུ་མ་དུང་ལ་སེར་འཛིན་བཞིན།
།ཇི་ལྟར་སྣང་དུས་ཉིད་ནས་གྲུབ་མ་མྱོང་།

།གཞི་མེད་རྟེན་མེད་ཐོག་མ་དབུས་ཐ་མེད།
།རང་བཞིན་གདོད་ནས་དག་པར་ཤེས་པར་བྱ།
།འདི་ལྟར་སྣང་སྲིད་སྣོད་བཅུད་ཆོས་རྣམས་ལ།
།གཟུང་བའི་ཡུལ་མེད་སྤྲུལ་པ་མིག་ཡོར་བཞིན།
།འཛིན་པའི་སེམས་མེད་པར་སྣང་དག་པ་འདྲ།
།གཟུང་འཛིན་གཉིས་མེད་འཁོར་བ་ཡོད་མ་མྱོང་།

།མེད་སྣང་འཁྲུལ་པ་རང་བཞིན་ཤེས་པས་གྲོལ།
།སྤང་བླང་རྒྱུ་འབྲས་རྐྱེན་སྣང་རང་དག་པས།
།གནས་ལུགས་དོན་ལ་རྒྱུ་འབྲས་འདས་ཤེས་བྱ།

Samsara is a false premise without the marks of existence.
Appearing without existing, it is empty of essence.
Its empty appearances are substanceless,
like strands of hair seen by diseased eyes,
Like a dream, a magical display, or a white conch
seen as yellow.
So from their very moment of appearing,
in whatever ways they have,
these visions have never been present at all.

Without basis, without support, without beginning, middle, or end,
Know that by nature [samsara] is pure from the beginning.
Within the entire scope of phenomena of worlds and beings,
Like conjured forms or hallucinations, there are no objects to grasp;
And like pure empty space there is no mind to grasp them.
And without these two – grasper and grasped –
samsara has never existed.

Nonexistent illusory appearances are released
when their nature is known.
Since rejection and acceptance, cause and effect,
and conditioned appearances are themselves pure,
Understand that the natural state really
is beyond cause and effect.

The Light of the Sun

།དེ་ཡི་རྟེན་གཞི་རིག་པ་བྱང་ཆུབ་སེམས།
།མྱ་ངན་འདས་དབྱིངས་ལྷུན་གྲུབ་ཆེན་པོ་ནི།
།དོན་དམ་བདེན་པ་གདོད་ནས་དག་པ་སྟེ།
།ཐོག་མ་དང་ནི་ཐ་མ་མེད་པའི་བདག
།རང་བཞིན་འོད་གསལ་ཟབ་ཞི་སྤྲོས་དང་བྲལ།
།ཡེ་ནས་རང་གནས་ཆོས་སྐུ་དྲི་མ་མེད།
།དུས་གསུམ་འཕོ་འགྱུར་མེད་པའི་ངོ་བོར་གནས།
།འདི་ནི་གཞི་དབྱིངས་རྡོ་རྗེ་སྙིང་པོ་སྟེ།
།གང་གིས་དེ་རྟོགས་གནས་ལུགས་ལྟ་བ་ཉིད།
།སྒྲོ་སྐུར་ཞི་བ་དོན་གྱི་སྙིང་པོར་རྟོགས།

།དྲི་མེད་སྒོམ་པ་འོད་གསལ་སྙིང་པོ་ནི།
།རྟོགས་པའི་ངང་ནས་བྱིང་རྒོད་སྤྲོས་དང་བྲལ།
།ཡེངས་མེད་བློ་བྲལ་ཡངས་པ་ཆེན་པོ་སྟེ།
།མཁའ་ལྟར་རྣམ་དག་རྒྱ་ཆད་ཕྱོགས་ལྷུང་མེད།
།བསམ་བརྗོད་དམིགས་པ་ཀུན་ལས་འདས་པ་ལགས།

།སྤྱོད་པ་གང་སྣང་བདེན་མེད་དག་པ་སྟེ།
།ནང་གི་འཛིན་པ་གང་ཤར་རང་གྲོལ་དང་།
།ཕྱི་རོལ་གཟུང་བ་རྨི་ལམ་སྒྱུ་མའི་ཚུལ།
།དོན་ལ་གཉིས་མེད་བླང་དོར་མེད་པར་སྤྱོད།

The base of all of this is *rigpa bodhichitta,*
The real condition beyond all suffering, the total state
of self-perfection.
This is the ultimate truth, primordial purity,
The true identity without beginning or end,
Natural luminous clarity, profound, peaceful,
and free of elaboration.
It is the primordially self-existing, stainless *dharmakaya*
That abides as the essence beyond the three times
of transition and change.
It is the Vajra essence, the real condition of the base,
And whoever realizes it has the authentic view
of the natural state,
The realization of the actual essence
wherein all affirmations and denials are pacified.

Stainless meditation, the essence of luminous clarity,
Is to be free of dullness, agitation, and proliferation of thoughts
while abiding within the state of knowledge,
An undistracted mind-free great openness
Totally pure like the sky, without any limitation or partiality,
Beyond all thought, expression, and objectification.

Whatever manifests is unreal and pure:
Inside, whatever grasping concepts arise self-liberate;
Outside, the objects of grasping are like a dream
or a magical display;
In reality, neither of these exist, so the conduct is to act
without accepting or rejecting.

The Light of the Sun

།གཟུང་འཛིན་ཉོན་མོངས་དགག།སྒྲུབ་ཆོས་རྣམས་ལ།
།སྐྱེས་པས་རང་གྲོལ་རང་བཞིན་ཤེས་པས་གྲོལ།
།གྲོལ་བས་ཡེ་རྫོགས་ཆོས་སྐུ་མཉམ་པའི་ངང་།
།འཁོར་བ་སྤངས་ནས་མྱ་ངན་འདས་མི་འཚོལ།

།གང་སྣང་དོན་གྱི་གསལ་འདེབས་མི་ཡོང་ལ།
།གང་ཤར་ཤེས་པ་རང་གྲོལ་ཆོས་སྐུའི་རྩལ།
།ཆུ་དང་རླབས་བཞིན་ཆོས་སྐུར་ཕྱམ་གཅིག་པོ
།འདི་ནི་མཐར་ཐུག་དོན་གྱི་དགོངས་པ་སྟེ།
།ལྟ་བའི་ཡང་རྩེ་རྫོགས་པ་ཆེན་པོ་ལགས།

།མདོར་ན་གང་ཞིག་ཇི་ལྟར་ཉམས་ལེན་ཀྱང་།
།བདག་འཛིན་རང་གྲོལ་ཉོན་མོངས་དབྱིངས་སུ་དག
།ཐམས་ཅད་ཐབས་ཀྱི་སྤྱོད་ལ་མཁས་པ་ནི།
།ལམ་གྱི་འཁྲུལ་པ་སེལ་ཞེས་བྱ་བར་བསྟན།

།དེ་ལྟར་ཆོས་རྒྱལ་རིན་ཆེན་གྲུ་བོ་ཆེས།
།མ་ལུས་སྐྱེ་རྒུ་སྲིད་མཚོ་རབ་བརྒལ་ནས།
།ཞི་བ་རིན་ཆེན་ཐར་པའི་གླིང་མཆོག་ཏུ།
།ཟག་མེད་ཞི་བདེའི་དགའ་སྟོན་མཐོང་བར་ཤོག

།ཆོས་བཞི་རིན་པོ་ཆེའི་ཕྲེང་བ་ལས།
།ལམ་འཁྲུལ་བ་སེལ་བའི་རབས་ཏེ་གསུམ་པའོ།

These phenomena – the grasper and the grasped, emotions,
    and concepts of negation and affirmation –
Are self-liberated upon arising;
    they are liberated by your knowing their nature.
Being liberated, they are the primordially perfect *dharmakaya* state
    of equality,
So do not turn away from samsara to seek nirvana.

Whatever appears is a mirror showing you the real nature,
And whatever arises within it is self-liberated awareness,
    the dynamic energy of *dharmakaya*.
Like water and waves, they are a single evenness within the *dharmakaya*.
This is the ultimate and actual state of knowledge,
The summit of all views, Total Perfection.

In short, whichever of these modes of practice you engage in,
Your ego grasping self-liberates, and your emotions
    are purified within the real condition.
Becoming adept at applying these methods to everything
Is what is meant by clearing away illusion on the path.

May the great jewel ship of this way of Dharma
Carry all beings without exception across the ocean of existence
And lead them to the precious state of peace,
    the supreme island of liberation,
To behold the festival of immaculate peace and bliss.

From *The Precious Mala of the Four Dharmas,* this is the third teaching, on clearing away illusion on the path.

The Light of the Sun

།དེ་ནས་འཁྲུལ་པ་ཡེ་ཤེས་དག་པ་ཡང་།
།གནས་སྐབས་མཐར་ཐུག་དོན་གྱི་རིམ་པ་ལས།

།དང་པོ་གནས་སྐབས་ཉམས་ལེན་ལམ་གྱི་དུས།
།ཟབ་མོའི་ཐབས་ཀྱིས་གོམས་པར་བྱས་པ་ལས།
།ཉོན་མོངས་གང་སྐྱེ་དབྱིངས་སུ་རྣམ་པར་དག
།རང་གསལ་ཡེ་ཤེས་མངོན་དུ་གྱུར་པ་ནི།
།འཁྲུལ་རྟོག་ཡེ་ཤེས་དབྱིངས་སུ་དག་ཅེས་བྱ།

།དེ་ཡང་ཐུན་མོང་ཁྱད་པར་བླ་མེད་ལ།
།བསྙེན་པའི་ཐབས་ཀྱིས་སོ་སོར་དབྱེ་བ་ནི།
།གཉེན་པོས་སྦྱངས་དང་ཐབས་ཀྱིས་བསྒྱུར་བ་དང་།
།རང་སར་རྣམ་གྲོལ་མ་སྤངས་དབྱིངས་སུ་དག
།གང་དག་འདོད་ལ་ཇི་ལྟར་བསྟན་ན་ཡང་།
།འགག་པ་ཉོན་མོངས་དག་པའི་དོན་དུ་གཅིག

།འདོད་ཆགས་ཞེ་སྡང་གཏི་མུག་ང་རྒྱལ་དང་།
།ཕྲག་དོག་སྐྱེས་པའི་རང་ས་ངོས་ཟིན་དུས།
།རང་བཞག་རང་གྲོལ་ཡེ་ཤེས་རྣམ་ལྔར་དག
།ཀུན་རྟོག་མེ་ལོང་ཆོས་དབྱིངས་མཉམ་པ་ཉིད།
།བྱ་བ་གྲུབ་པའི་ཡེ་ཤེས་ཆེན་པོ་རུ།
།དུག་ལྔའི་འཁྲུལ་པ་གནས་སྐབས་དག་ཅེས་བྱ།

Then, illusion is purified as wisdom.
This purification has a provisional stage
and a final, definitive stage.

First, on the provisional stage of the path of practice,
Having become accustomed to profound skillful methods,
Whatever emotions arise are completely purified
in the real condition
And self-illuminating wisdom manifests directly.
This is called the purification of illusory concepts
within the real condition of wisdom.

This can be achieved in reliance upon the methods
Of the common, special, or unexcelled approach:
Respectively, illusion can be cleansed away by means of antidotes,
transformed through special methods,
Or liberated in its own state and purified in the real condition
without being abandoned.
But whichever of these ways you are drawn to and able to train in,
They are the same in that they bring the emotions to an end
by purifying them.

When you recognize the ground from which attachment, anger,
ignorance, pride, and jealousy all emerge,
By relaxing in your own state [the emotions] self-liberate
and are purified as the five wisdoms.
This is called the provisional purification, in which the illusions of
the five poisons are purified
As the great wisdoms of total discernment, the mirror,
the real condition of phenomena, equality,
and the accomplishment of actions.

The Light of the Sun

།མཐར་ཐུག་ཁམས་ཀྱི་གློ་བུར་དྲི་བྲལ་ཏེ།
།བྱང་ཆུབ་ཞི་བ་རྟུལ་བྲལ་བརྙེས་པ་ན།
།དབྱིངས་ཀྱི་རང་བཞིན་ཅི་འདྲ་མངོན་དུ་གྱུར།
།སྐུ་གསུམ་ཆོས་སྐུ་རོ་གཅིག་ཡེ་ཤེས་བརྙེས།

།དག་པ་གཉིས་ལྡན་དབྱིངས་ཀྱི་སྐུ་ཞེས་བྱ།
།རྒྱལ་བ་ཉིད་ལས་གཞན་གྱི་ཡུལ་མིན་པ།
།ཆོས་དང་ལོངས་སྤྱོད་སྤྲུལ་པའི་སྐུ་གསུམ་ཉིད།
།ཡེ་ཤེས་དང་བཅས་ངོ་བོ་ཉིད་སྐུས་བསྡུས།

།རྟག་ཁྱབ་འདུས་མ་བྱས་ཤིང་འཕོ་འགྱུར་མེད།
།ཡིད་བཞིན་ནོར་བུ་ཆོས་སྐུའི་དབྱིངས་ན་བཞུགས།
།དེ་ཉིད་ངང་ལས་ཡེ་ཤེས་ཕྲིན་ལས་སྐུ།
།ལོངས་སྤྱོད་རྫོགས་དང་སྤྲུལ་སྐུའི་རོལ་པ་ནི།
།སར་གནས་རྣམས་དང་འགྲོ་གཞན་སྣང་བ་ཡང་།
།རྒྱལ་བའི་བྱིན་རླབས་གདུལ་བྱའི་བསོད་ནམས་མཐུ།
།ཚོགས་དོན་དག་ལས་དེ་ལྟར་སྣང་བ་ལས།
།སྲིད་པ་ཇི་སྲིད་ཕྲིན་ལས་རྒྱུན་མི་འཆད།
།ནོར་བུ་དཔག་བསམ་ལྗོན་ཤིང་རེ་བ་སྐོང་།
།འདི་ནི་འཕྲུལ་པ་ཡེ་ཤེས་དག་ཅེས་བྱ།

In the definitive stage, when you are freed from the stains
that temporarily obscured your nature,
And attain the immaculate peace of awakening,
The nature of the real condition manifests directly,
just as it is,
And you attain the wisdom in which the three *kayas*
are of a single taste as *dharmakaya.*

This is called the *kaya* of the real condition endowed
with twofold purity,
And is the domain of the conquerors alone.
The *dharmakaya, sambhogakaya,* and *nirmanakaya,*
together with their wisdoms,
Are subsumed within the *svabhavikakaya.*

Permanent, all-pervasive, uncompounded, without
transition or change,
This wish-granting jewel abides in the real condition
of *dharmakaya.*
From within that state, by the combined force
of the conquerors' blessings and disciples' merit,
The *kayas* of wisdom activity – the displays of *sambhogakaya*
and *nirmanakaya* –
Appear respectively to those abiding on the *bhumis*
and to ordinary beings,
Manifesting enlightened activity ceaselessly
for as long as samsara remains,
Fulfilling all hopes like a wish-granting jewel
or a wish-granting tree.
This is called the purification of illusion as wisdom.

The Light of the Sun

།དེ་ལྟར་དོན་ཟབ་སྙིང་པོའི་ཏྲ་བདུན་གྱིས།
།ཡིད་མཁའི་ལམ་ནས་གདུལ་བྱའི་འཛིག་རྟེན་དུ།
།ཚིག་དོན་རྣམ་བཀྲའི་འོད་སྟོང་འཕྲོ་བ་ཡིས།
།འགྲོ་ཀུན་མ་རིག་མུན་པ་སངས་བར་ཤོག

།ཆོས་བཞི་རིན་པོ་ཆེའི་ཕྲེང་བ་ལས།
།འཁྲུལ་པ་ཡེ་ཤེས་སུ་དག་པའི་རབས་ཏེ་བཞི་པའོ།

།ཚུལ་འདི་བློ་གྲོས་ཡངས་པའི་ཁང་བཟང་ནས།
།ཐོས་བསམ་སྒོམ་པའི་འབྱོར་པས་རབ་བརྒྱན་པ།
།རང་གཞན་དོན་གཉིས་དགའ་སྟོན་འགྱེད་པ་དེས།
།མདོ་རྒྱུད་མན་ངག་སྙིང་པོའི་དོན་བཞིན་བཀོད།

།དགེ་བ་འདི་ཡིས་བདག་དང་འགྲོ་བ་ཀུན།
།ཚེ་འདིར་སྲིད་པའི་རི་བོ་ཕྱིར་བསྐྱིལ་ནས།
།བྱང་ཆུབ་ཞི་བ་རྡུལ་བྲལ་མཆོག་ཐོབ་སྟེ།
།རང་གཞན་དོན་གཉིས་རྫོགས་པའི་སངས་རྒྱས་ཤོག

།དོན་གསལ་གངས་རི་རྒྱ་ཆེར་མཛེས་པའི་གནས།
།རབ་དཀར་ཡོན་ཏན་ཕྱོགས་ཀྱི་ཐ་གྲུར་ཁྱབ།
།གསུང་རབ་རིན་ཆེན་སྙིང་པོའི་གནས་འཚེར་བས།
།དད་ལྡན་སྐྱེ་བོའི་ཚོགས་རྣམས་དགའ་བར་མཛོད།

May this seven-horse-drawn sun of the profound essential meaning
Traverse its path through the sky of the minds of disciples,
And shine into their world a thousand light rays
of beautiful words and meanings
That cleanse away the darkness of ignorance from the minds
of all beings.

From *The Precious Mala of the Four Dharmas,* this is the fourth teaching, on the purification of illusion as wisdom.

Within the palace of vast intelligence,
Well ornamented with the riches of listening,
reflection, and meditation,
I have set out this delightful feast of Dharma
that benefits both myself and others
In accord with the essential meaning
of the sutras, tantras, and *upadeshas.*

By this merit, may I and all beings
Crush the mountain of samsara to the ground in this very life,
And attain the supreme immaculate peace of awakening,
The total enlightenment that fulfills the aim of self and others.

The vast and beautiful abode of snow mountains of clear meaning
Spreads pure and precious qualities
to the limits [of space] in all directions.
[Like this,] may the brilliant light of these [four] themes
of the precious essence of excellent speech
Bring joy to those endowed with faith.

།ཆོས་བཞི་རིན་པོ་ཆེའི་ཕྲེང་བ་ཞེས་བྱ་བ། །ཐེག་པ་མཆོག་གི་རྒྱལ་འབྱོར་པ་ཀུན་མཁྱེན་ངག་གི་དབང་པོས་གངས་རི་ཁྲོད་དཀར་གྱི་མགུལ། མེ་ཏོག་སྤྲིན་གྱི་སྙིང་མོས་ཚལ་གྱི་ནང་། ཀུན་ཏུ་བཟང་པོའི་ཁང་བཟང་ཟླ་བ་ཆུ་ཤེལ་གྱིས་འཚོར་བར་སྦྱར་བ་སྟེ་རེ་ཞིག་རྫོགས་སོ། །ཕྱོགས་དུས་ཀུན་ཏུ་བདེ་ཆེན་གྱི་ཆར་བསྐལ་པ་རྫོགས་ལྡན་གྱི་དུས་བཞིན་དུ་འབབ་པས་བསམ་རྒྱུའི་རེ་བ་ཐམས་ཅད་འགྲུབ་པར་གྱུར་ཅིག།

In the excellent house of Samantabhadra, within a pleasure grove of flowers and mist on the slope of White Skull Snow Mountain, this *Precious Mala of the Four Dharmas* was written down all at once, by the shimmering light of the waxing moon, by Kunkhyen Ngaggi Wangpo – Omniscient Lord of Speech – a yogin of the supreme vehicle.

In all places and at all times, may a rain of great bliss descend, just as in the aeon of perfection, bringing all our hopes to fruition.

Introduction to the Teaching

THIS IS AN EXPLANATION of Longchenpa's text called *The Precious Mala of the Four Dharmas*,[1] which he composed on the basis of the Four Dharmas of Gampopa.[2] As one of the heart disciples of the great eleventh-century yogin Milarepa, Gampopa is considered particularly important by all followers of the Kagyüd tradition. The teaching of the Four Dharmas arose through Gampopa's personal knowledge and understanding, and he used these four points to introduce the essence of all the Dharma teachings of Buddha Shakyamuni to his students. For this reason, this teaching has become widely diffused throughout the Kagyüd tradition.

Longchenpa was one of the greatest masters of the Nyingma tradition and, in particular, one of the most important teachers of Dzogchen. He saw these Four Dharmas of Gampopa as a wonderful teaching, and while he was staying in solitary retreat, at a time when he was already an advanced practitioner himself, he composed this short text.

---

1 See bibliography.

2 See Jampa Mackenzie Stewart, *The Life of Gampopa* and *The Life of Longchenpa*, as well as Chögyal Namkhai Norbu, *The Temple of the Great Contemplation*, for biographies of these and other masters mentioned in this book.

The teaching of the Four Dharmas begins on the Sutrayana level of teachings, and both Longchenpa and Gampopa essentially present these two topics from the same approach. But the third and fourth Dharmas deal very much with higher levels of teachings, and here there is a difference. Gampopa's knowledge came primarily from his application of the practice of Mahamudra and the Vajrayana teachings of the Kagyüd tradition, so this is what he emphasizes in his teaching. Longchenpa also presents the path of transformation in this text, mainly according to the Nyingma tradition, but his explanation of the essence of the teaching is related to Dzogchen. He wrote this text to show how these four principles can be understood and applied in the context of the Dzogchen teachings.

The Lineage of This Teaching

I received this teaching from Khyenrab Chökyi Wözer (1889–1958), the teacher of the monastic college I attended in Tibet when I was young. Khyenrab Chökyi Wözer was not only a teacher of philosophy but also one of the three most important students of the great Dzogchen master Zhenga Rinpoche (1871–1927),[3] from whom he received this teaching of Longchenpa. Zhenga Rinpoche's teacher was Wönpo Tendzin Norbu (1851–unknown), who was in turn one of the most important students of Dza Paltrul Rinpoche (1808–1887), another highly influential master in the lineage of the Dzogchen teachings. His teacher, Jigmed Gyalwai Nyugu (1765–1842), was a direct student of the famous teacher Jigmed Lingpa (1730–1798), who received many teachings and transmissions directly from Longchenpa in a series of pure visions and then unified many different lineages of the Dzogchen

3 Also known as Khenpo Zhenga or Zhenphen Chökyi Nangwa.

teachings. So this is the lineage through which I received this teaching. Whenever we receive any teaching, and particularly a formal teaching, it is very important to know its lineage.

The Lineage of the Dzogchen Transmission

While this text explains many aspects of the Hinayana, Mahayana, and Vajrayana, it is mainly connected to the lineage of the Dzogchen teachings. Longchenpa does give a brief explanation of the two stages in Vajrayana practice – the development stage and completion stage – but without any concrete instructions on how we can apply these two stages. This is because we should receive a Vajrayana initiation before hearing detailed instructions on how to apply these stages, and even then, the instructions are so detailed and complex that it takes many months to learn everything. Even a master as great and well studied as Longchenpa cannot explain how to apply these stages of Vajrayana practice in only a few words. What he does explain here in a very concrete and clear way, however, is Dzogchen.

Dzogchen has a precise lineage of transmission, and it is important to understand that this transmission is like the life of the Dzogchen teachings. Therefore, if we want to apply the Dzogchen teachings, we should receive the Dzogchen transmission of Guruyoga. Otherwise these teachings will not function for us. Receiving transmission connects us to the Dzogchen lineage all the way back to Garab Dorje,[4] the origin of this transmission in our dimension and our epoch.

In ancient times, before Garab Dorje, many Dzogchen masters taught in our dimension, but all that now remains of their teachings are

4 Garab Dorje of Oddiyana is generally considered to have been born 360 years after the *parinirvana* of Buddha Shakyamuni.

a few words. This is because we live in time, and in time our situation is always changing. For example, during the Cultural Revolution in Tibet, even if someone just moved their mouth the Chinese police would accuse them of chanting Buddhist mantras. This is one example, but millions of situations like these have existed in our samsaric condition in the course of time. It could be that the transmissions and teachings of these earlier teachers continued for hundreds or even thousands of years, but eventually almost all of these teachings disappeared.

What now remains of these ancient teachings is only what we call *nyengyüd*, or oral transmissions, a few words passed on by mouth through the ages. For example, an oral transmission from a tantra of Manjushri is, "The single eye of wisdom is pure."[5] Even when the rest of that teaching had completely vanished, this one line remained and a teacher would secretly whisper it to his student, and then the student would keep these words in his heart and try to understand their meaning. Eventually he would pass this *nyengyüd* on to his own student.

Then Garab Dorje manifested in our dimension and transmitted all the Dzogchen teachings of the ancient teachers in the past that had vanished over time. For this reason we consider Garab Dorje the first Dzogchen teacher in our epoch. Everything we can learn now within the Dzogchen teachings of Semde, Longde, and Upadesha[6] come from Garab Dorje. They were passed on by his main student Manjushrimitra and by various masters in Oddiyana, where Garab Dorje lived and taught, as well as by important masters in India.

---

5 ཡེ་ཤེས་མིག་གཅིག་དྲི་མ་མེད།

6 The three series of Dzogchen teachings (series of Mind, series of Space, and series of Secret Instructions).

These teachings were later brought to Tibet and transmitted by Guru Padmasambhava,[7] and later still by Vairochana, one of his students who, along with several others, also translated the original Dzogchen texts into the Tibetan language. Padmasambhava and Vairochana had many students, so the Dzogchen transmission passed from them to their own students, and this has continued without interruption until today.

---

7 The great master from Oddiyana who brought the Buddhist teachings to Tibet in the eighth century.

Title and Introductory Verses

།རྒྱ་གར་སྐད་དུ། །ཙ་ཏུར་དྷརྨ་རཏྣ་མཱ་ལ་ནཱ་མ། །བོད་སྐད་དུ། །ཆོས་བཞི་རིན་པོ་ཆེའི་ཕྲེང་བ་ཞེས་བྱ་བ།

In the language of India, *catur-dharma-ratnamāla-nāma.*
In the language of Tibet, *chö zhi rinpochei trengwa she chawa.*

IN GENERAL, Tibetan Buddhists have the idea that the most important texts of their tradition come from India and were written in the Sanskrit language. For this reason, when a text comes from India and is then translated into Tibetan, the translator always includes its original Sanskrit title as an indication of its origins.

Some Tibetan masters have followed this convention of including a Sanskrit title even when a text is originally composed in Tibet by Tibetans. The great master Sakya Pandita did this, as did Longchenpa. Their intention was not to create confusion but to indicate that these texts are just as precious, of the same quality, as the writings of the great pandits of India.

Longchenpa gives the title of this text as *The Precious Mala of the Four Dharmas.* Four Dharmas refers to the Four Dharmas of Gampopa. In general, a *dharma* can refer to any phenomenon or thing. But when we speak of the Buddha's Dharma, we are referring specifically to Buddha's teachings, whose purpose is the discovery of the real nature of all phenomena. The word *mala* is in the title because in addition to four basic topics, within each topic the text contains many points related to different levels of the teachings.[8] So even though it is a short teaching, it is something highly useful for developing our knowledge.

།སངས་རྒྱས་དང་བྱང་ཆུབ་སེམས་དཔའ་ཐམས་ཅད་ལ་ཕྱག་འཚལ་ལོ།

Homage to all buddhas and bodhisattvas!

།གང་གི་རང་བཞིན་ཆོས་སྐུའི་མཁའ་དབྱིངས་ལ།
།ངེས་པ་ལྔ་ལྡན་གཟུགས་སྐུའི་དཀྱིལ་འཁོར་རྒྱས།
།མཛད་པའི་ཟེར་གྱིས་གདུལ་བྱའི་པདྨོ་འཛུམ།
།བདེ་གཤེགས་ཉི་མ་དད་བརྒྱའི་གཙུག་གིས་མཆོད།

Within the dharmakaya dimension of space
Unfolds the rupakaya mandala endowed with
  five certainties,
Its rays of activity causing lotus disciples to blossom.
To you who have this nature, sun-like Sugata, I make offerings
  with the highest faith.

We begin by paying homage in a general way to all buddhas and all Mahayana masters. Then we have a verse that is also for paying homage, in more detail, to the three *kayas*: to the physical level of *nirmanakaya* manifestations, to the form dimensions of *sambhogakaya*, and to the base of both of these, the *dharmakaya*, which is just like space.

Within that space, the form dimensions manifest with five certainties. These five certainties are the five conditions that are always present as characteristics of *sambhogakaya* manifestations: the certain place, or

---

8 A *mala* is a rosary, usually consisting of 108 beads, used in Buddhist prayer and practice.

dimension; the certain time, or occasion; the certain teacher; the certain teaching that this teacher communicates; and the certain assembly that receives this teaching. All *sambhogakaya* manifestations have these five characteristics in a precise way.

Then there are the *nirmanakaya* emanations. These are not perfect in the same way as the manifestations of *sambhogakaya*, but they also have their precise qualities and symbols. For example, every sutra begins with verses that represent these same five characteristics, starting with, "Thus have I heard. At one time..." and so forth. Here the *nirmanakaya* buddhas are described as being like the rays of the sun: their activities of teaching and guiding beings cause the minds of students to open with understanding, just like lotus flowers blossoming.

So we pay homage to these three dimensions of the Buddha, which are like the sun with its rays shining in space.

།རྒྱལ་བའི་ཆོས་ཚུལ་རིན་ཆེན་དཔག་བསམ་ཤིང་།
།མ་ལུས་སྲིད་ཞིའི་གདུང་སྐྱོབ་བསིལ་གྲིབ་དེར།
།དད་ལྡན་སྐྱེ་རྒུ་རིམ་གྱིས་འཇུག་པའི་ཚུལ།
།རྣམ་བཞིའི་ཡོན་ཏན་ལྡན་ཚོགས་བཤད་ཀྱིས་ཉོན།

The teaching of the Conqueror is a precious
wish-granting tree,
Giving shelter from the searing heat of samsara and nirvana.
All of you with faith, listen as I explain how to enter,
step by step,
Into the refreshing shade of this tree
with four precious qualities.

When the weather is hot and the sun is strong, if you can find a nice tree and stay under it, you feel cool and refreshed. This teaching of the Four Dharmas is like a marvelous, wish-granting tree. Although we are suffering in the heat of samsara, we can enter the shade of this tree and take shelter. So Longchenpa says he will explain how we can do this, and we should listen well.

The First Dharma:
Turning Your Mind to the Dharma

།གང་ཞིག་མཐའ་མེད་འཁོར་བའི་རྒྱ་མཚོ་ལས།
།བརྒལ་འདོད་རྣམས་ཀྱིས་ཐོག་མར་བསམ་བྱ་བ།
།ཐར་པའི་ཆོས་དེ་ཞི་བདེ་བསྒྲུབ་པའི་ཕྱིར།
།ད་རེས་ཚེ་འདིར་ཡོངས་སུ་འབད་པར་བྱ།

Those who long to go beyond the endless ocean of samsara
First must think, "This time, in this life,
I will truly apply myself to the liberating Dharma
In order to realize peace and happiness."

SAMSARA IS LIKE a great ocean. When we see this – that transmigration is infinite and that the suffering we experience within it is also infinite – we will naturally want to cross this ocean, and the first step is to look at our situation and decide that this moment, this life, is the time to really do our best to attain liberation. Why? Because it is in this moment that we actually have the opportunity to do this: we are receiving the teachings that we can use to attain that liberation, and we have all the circumstances necessary to follow and apply these teachings.

The first of the Four Dharmas is to direct our minds to the Dharma. Dharma is something very important for all sentient beings, both for attaining liberation and, on a provisional level, for living a more comfortable life. This is what Longchenpa means when he says we should work to accomplish peace and happiness by applying the liberating Dharma. The Tibetan words for peace and happiness, *shi* and *de,* are often used in common speech as a single word that means peace in a general sense, but here there is a precise meaning with two aspects. *Shi* refers to provisional, conditioned peace and happiness, in the sense of having relative freedom from confusion and difficulties; it is a calm state that is free of ordinary hardships. *De* means that, having found this temporary state of peace, we use the opportunity to liberate ourselves from samsara and attain the definitive, unconditioned happiness of enlightenment. This is the real meaning of *shi de.*

Yet even though we can have relative peace and ultimate happiness in this very life by practicing the Dharma, only a very small number of people actually practice. How many of the inhabitants of an entire city or country follow the Dharma? For example, consider the number of people who would rather watch football than learn and apply the Dharma: when there is an important football match, sometimes millions of people are watching, but when an important Dharma teaching is given, the number of people present is always quite limited. This is because most people do not actually understand how valuable and important the Dharma is for them.

So before anything else, we need to direct our minds to the Dharma by seeing its value and necessity. To help us accomplish this, all traditions and schools of Tibetan Buddhism begin by introducing students to four considerations that we call the four mindfulnesses, or the four thoughts that turn the mind from samsara. For this reason, whenever we teach the Four Dharmas of Gampopa, the first Dharma is always taught on the basis of these four mindfulnesses.

The Four Mindfulnesses

The first of the four mindfulnesses is to recognize how precious and rare our human condition is. Second, we must recognize that although this condition of ours is very precious, we will lose it one day because we exist in time, and whatever is in time is impermanent. Third, we observe that as time passes we are always distracted by our emotions, and when we act on these emotions we continually produce negative karma. Then, as the result of our accumulation of this negative karma, we experience infinite suffering in samsara; this is the fourth mindfulness.

Some traditions approach these four as topics by studying them in an intellectual way. But it is not so important to learn all the details and logical arguments. What matters is to come to an understanding of their real sense, so that this knowledge becomes concrete and we are able to keep that presence in our daily lives; this is why they are called four kinds of mindfulness.

།རྙེད་པར་དཀའ་ཞིང་འཇིག་པར་སླ་བའི་ལུས།
།དལ་འབྱོར་གྲུ་བོ་ཐོབ་དུས་མ་འབད་ན།
།སྲིད་པའི་མཚོ་ལས་ནམ་ཡང་མི་ཐར་ཤིང་།
།སྣ་ཚོགས་སྡུག་བསྔལ་མང་ལྡན་རྒྱུན་མི་འཆད།

If you do not strive for this now that you have
 obtained the ship
Of freedom and advantage – this human body,
 so difficult to find and so easily destroyed –
You will never escape the ocean of samsara,
And its stream of sufferings in all their variety
 will never be cut off.

Our present condition is like a ship that can carry us beyond the ocean of transmigration, and this is true because in our condition we have the eighteen freedoms and advantages.

First, having the eight freedoms means we are free from eight conditions that would deprive us of the opportunity to practice the Dharma. We have not taken birth in a hell realm or in the *preta*[9] realm, where we would be too overwhelmed by pain to learn or apply the Dharma. We have not been born as animals who have no power to understand the Dharma teachings. We were not born in the god realms, where we would have a long and easy life but be too caught up in the enjoyments of our condition to even think about practicing the Dharma.

Then, even if we are born as humans, there are places where the very word Dharma does not exist. On our planet Earth many places like this still exist, but we have not been born in that kind of place. Then there are people who have received some education and may even have learned some Dharma but reject it and hold contrary ideas instead, and we are not like this either. Also, we have not taken birth in a dimension where no buddha has manifested. For example, in our world, Buddha Shakyamuni has come and given the teachings of Dharma, and these teachings are still alive. This is why we consider that our dimension is the *nirmanakaya* pure land of Buddha Shakyamuni. But in many dimensions no buddhas have come and taught, and therefore these are places providing no opportunity to attain liberation. Finally, even if we are born in a place where a buddha has taught, and even if we have interest, if our faculties are impaired – for example, if we cannot hear or communicate – we will not be able to easily understand or receive the teachings. So these are the eight unfree states, and being free of them is called having the eight freedoms.

9 Hungry ghost.

Just as we are free from all of these limiting conditions, we also have ten advantages or positive conditions that enable us to practice the Dharma. Five of these have to do with ourselves and five with our dimension and circumstances. The five related to ourselves are that we have been born as humans, that we live in a place where the Dharma exists, that all our faculties are complete, that we do not live in a way that puts us at odds with the Dharma, and that we have interest in the Buddha and his teachings. The five related to our circumstances are that a buddha has come to our world, that he has taught the Dharma, that his teachings still remain, that there is a community that continues to apply these teachings, and that there are teachers who have the kindness to guide us so we can learn and apply these teachings ourselves.

If you want to learn about all these points one by one, you can find many books on the subject. But this is not as important as it is to simply compare your condition to that of a dog, for example, and examine how different your situation really is in terms of the ability to understand and apply the Dharma. Or you can compare yourself to a large animal, like an elephant: compared to us, an elephant is much stronger, but as humans we have the capacity to destroy an entire country, or to totally destroy ourselves by creating the causes for infinite samsara. We also have the capacity to do the opposite and achieve total realization in our lifetime.

These are the characteristics of a precious human life with all its freedoms and advantages. So rather than chanting verses or learning logical arguments about this, it is much more important to always remember that in this moment, in this life, we have a very rare situation, and if we do not do our best and use it to attain liberation, we will never cross the ocean of samsara but will just continue to have different kinds of suffering without interruption.

།སྐྱེ་ཤིའི་ཆུ་བོ་པ་མཐའ་མི་མངོན་ཞིང་།
།ན་ཆའི་ལྦུ་ཕྲེང་ཀུན་ནས་འཁྲུགས་པའི་གནས།
།ཉོན་མོངས་དུས་རླབས་སྲིད་རྩེའི་མཐའ་ཁྱབ་པའི།
།མཚོ་ཆེན་མི་བཟོད་འཇིགས་སུ་ཐུམ་པར་རྩེན།

You will be tossed around in terror on this vast,
unbearable sea,
With its endless currents of birth and death,
Its froth of illness and old age converging from all sides,
Its tides of emotion rising to even the peak of existence.

As human beings, we are subject to four types of suffering that can be considered universal. Of course, in our human dimension, we may experience many different kinds of suffering according to our circumstances, but these four are the most basic sufferings of our human condition. First is the suffering of birth: when we are in our mother's womb for nine months and our physical body is slowly developing, there is no light, nowhere to move. Our mother eats and drinks things that sometimes give us a sensation of burning, sometimes of cold. When she moves around it is painful for us. Finally, the moment of birth itself is an ordeal for both our mother and ourselves.

Then we get bigger and bigger, we grow up, and finally become old. Nobody wants to grow old, but whether we want to or not, time passes and it just happens. As old people, we get very heavy illnesses that can kill us.

Of course, we do not have to be old to become ill: some people have heavy illnesses throughout their lives. Also, we do not need to be old or sick in order to die. Many people of all ages die suddenly in accidents. In any case, all of us die; none of us remain on Earth forever. Everybody knows that it is not possible to remain forever. Many people think, "I want to live one hundred years." But after one hundred years, what happens? You die. Nobody thinks, "I want to live forever." They know this is impossible.

Also, the number of times we must go through this process of birth and death is infinite. In our samsaric condition, we die and are reborn, die and are reborn, again and again. The flow of birth and death is like a river, always moving ahead. And in this river many bubbles are always manifesting, just as our physical body gets many kinds of illness, as we age, and so on. Also, there are always many waves of emotions – big waves, small waves – there is no limit to the kinds of emotions that continually arise.

Sometimes we might think things are not so bad, that samsara also has some nice things to offer. For example, if we go on a holiday we can enjoy many things, and that is also samsara. But even then, our minds never stop with desires and negative emotions, so we are always accumulating negative karma. We are always doing so much that later brings the consequence of infinite transmigration. Even if we see a beautiful flower, this immediately causes us to fall into attachment and we become distracted by that, which means we are producing negative karma. So it is very important to know that there really is no happiness in samsara.

།གང་ཞིག་ཐོས་ནས་སྐྱེ་ཤི་རྒྱུན་ཆད་དེ།
།བདེ་ཆེན་མཆོག་དང་ནམ་ཡང་མི་འབྲལ་བ།
།ཞི་བའི་ཆོས་མཆོག་རིན་ཆེན་གྲུ་བཟང་གིས།
།སྲིད་གསུམ་ཉོན་མོངས་ཆུ་གཏེར་བརྒལ་ཕྱིར་འབད།

But whoever, having heard [the Dharma], cuts the stream
of birth and death,
Will never be parted from unsurpassable great bliss.

So strive to cross beyond the sea of the three realms
of emotion
On the precious jewel ship, the supreme Dharma of peace.

Our only chance to interrupt this cycle is to hear and understand the teachings of the Dharma. This Dharma is like a good boat that can carry us beyond the three realms – the realm of desire, of form, and without form – which include all the dimensions of existence generally called the six realms of samsara. So even though, in general, there is no way to interrupt samsara, it actually is possible for us to do this if we have the Dharma.

།ད་རེས་ཐར་ལམ་བྱང་ཆུབ་མ་བསྒྲུབས་ན།
།ཕྱི་ནས་བདེ་འགྲོའི་མིང་ཡང་མི་གྲགས་ཤིང་།
།ངན་སོང་མཐའ་མེད་གཅིག་ནས་གཅིག་བརྒྱུད་དེ།
།གཏན་དུ་འཁོར་བའི་གནས་ལས་ཐར་ཐབས་མེད།

If you fail to accomplish awakening on the path
of liberation this time,
In future lives you will never even hear the names of the joyful realms,
Passing from one state of limitless misery to the next
With no means of ever escaping samsara.

We know that the reason samsara continues indefinitely for so many sentient beings is that they never have the conditions of freedom or the opportunity to interrupt its cycle. But if we do not know how to use our precious human condition to attain total realization now, later on the fruits of our negative karma will manifest and we will once again become just like these other beings, circling around endlessly with no way to liberate ourselves.

It will not be easy to find another human birth like the one we have now, because this kind of birth depends on positive karma, and in general we have so much negative karma that we are much more likely to be born in the lower states of existence. If we compare the number of humans to the number of animals in our world, including fish, insects, and so on, we can easily see how much more common it is to take birth as an animal than as a human. Of course, compared to the number of *pretas* and hell beings, we are even fewer.

So we must be aware. Samsara is infinite: there are so many beings who have no opportunity to end their cycle of transmigration, and if we pass our lives in distraction we might end up in that situation ourselves. So instead we should do our best to create an actual fruit of our Dharma practice in this life. Not only will this help us, but it will also give us the possibility to help others.

།དེ་བས་བློ་དང་ལྡན་པའི་སྐྱེ་བོ་རྣམས།
།དལ་དང་འབྱོར་བའི་མི་ལུས་ཐོབ་དུས་འདིར།
།སྙིང་ནས་བརྩོན་པས་ཕན་བདེ་བསྒྲུབ་པར་བྱ།
།དེས་ནི་རང་གཞན་དོན་གཉིས་འགྲུབ་པར་འགྱུར།

Therefore, those of you with keen intelligence,
Now that you have a human condition of freedom
    and advantage,
Must strive with all your heart to accomplish benefit
    and happiness:
This will fulfill both your own aim and that of others.

So for this reason, if we have some understanding of our situation, we will see that at this moment we have a very precious opportunity. As we have explained, if we do our best to apply the Dharma in daily life, provisionally we can obtain the peace and benefit we need in our relative condition, and definitively we can attain liberation from samsara. This means we can bring great benefit to ourselves and also to others.

།དལ་འབྱོར་ཐོབ་ཀྱང་ཡིད་བརྟན་འགའ་མེད་དེ།
།ཐམས་ཅད་མི་བརྟན་འགྱུར་ཞིང་སྙིང་པོ་མེད།
།སྐད་ཅིག་མི་རྟག་འཇིག་པའི་ཆོས་ཅན་ཏེ།
།མྱུར་དུ་འཆི་ཞེས་སྙིང་ནས་བསམ་པར་བྱ།

But even having gained these freedoms and advantages,
there is no security:
Everything is unstable, changeable, without essence,
Momentary, impermanent, subject to destruction.
So think, from deep within your heart, "Soon I will die."

With the first mindfulness, we recognize the opportunity of being human, and we try to keep this knowledge present in our minds at all times. But we must also recognize that this condition is impermanent and will end: this is the second mindfulness.

Our circumstances exist in time, and time is always passing, so our circumstances are always changing, day after day. For example, when two young people fall in love, at first they might even feel as if they have become united, like one person, and cannot imagine that the love they feel will ever change. But after two, three, or four years have passed, they might begin to feel uncomfortable, discovering that they also have many differences in their points of view, and so forth. Maybe they even get married and have some children, but still they do not feel the way they did before, and eventually they might start to think, "This was the wrong thing to do. We made a mistake and should separate."

So then they get a divorce, and after that they think they will not make the same mistakes again.

But after one or two years, they fall in love with other people, thinking, "This time it is different. This person and I really have the same way of seeing things and the same approach to life." Maybe they will feel this way for some months or years, but later on, this couple will also begin to feel uncomfortable together, and eventually they may not even feel like sleeping in the same bed. Finally they will not want to stay in the same house, and they separate, again feeling that this time they have learned something.

In fact, many people do this over and over again, always feeling that they have "learned something this time." In our modern society, we can see how many children have divorced parents. All of this is due to ordinary emotions, and does not produce happiness but only suffering, either directly or indirectly. Unfortunately, if it produces suffering indirectly it takes some time to discover what is really going on. We must understand that there is nothing that is not like this. From one second to the next, everything is continuously changing because nothing has a stable or permanent essence. It is truly important for us to have this awareness.

In terms of our own death, there are three things to consider. First, it is one hundred percent certain that some day we will die. Second, we can never be certain of how we will die. So many possible causes of death exist in our dimension and we are exposed to all of them, just like a flame that has been lit outdoors. Finally, none of us can know when the conditions for our death will manifest. For example, a young person might think they will not die as soon as an older person, but I am an old man and I have already seen many young people die before me. So we must understand that these three principles are our real condition. And, in particular, we must have an awareness that this opportunity we have now – our precious human condition – will certainly end, but we do not know when or how this will happen.

།འདི་ལྟར་སྣོད་ཀྱི་འཇིག་རྟེན་ཐམས་ཅད་ཀྱང་།
།མེ་བདུན་ཆུ་གཅིག་རླུང་གིས་འཇོར་བའི་ཚེ།
།སྤྲ་རྩེའི་ལྷག་མ་ཙམ་ཡང་ཡོང་མེད་པར།
།ཐམས་ཅད་སྟོང་སྟེ་ནམ་མཁའ་གཅིག་ཏུ་འགྱུར།

This entire world, the vessel,
Will be emptied and turned to a single space
With not even the tip of a hair remaining
When it is obliterated by seven fires, one flood, and wind.

The globe we live on is composed of the five physical elements, which are related to our karmic vision. So is our entire universe. Eventually the elements of fire, water, and wind destroy our entire dimension and everything becomes just empty space where everything is gone and nothing even as small as the tip of a single hair remains.

།བཅུད་རྣམས་མི་རྟག་འགྲོ་བ་གཡོ་བ་སྟེ།
།ལྷ་དང་ལྷ་མིན་མི་དང་དུད་འགྲོ་དང་།
།ཡི་དྭགས་དམྱལ་བའི་སེམས་ཅན་ཇི་སྙེད་ཀྱང་།
།དུས་མཐར་འཆི་འཕོ་སྐྱེ་བའི་ཆུ་བོར་བྱིང་།

Its contents, the impermanent beings who move within it –
Devas, asuras, humans, animals, hungry ghosts, and beings
of hell:
When their time comes, each one sinks down
Into the waters of death, transmigration, and rebirth.

Also, all sentient beings living within these impermanent dimensions of the six realms of samsara are themselves impermanent: no matter how long they live, eventually they all die and take rebirth in another condition.

As we have already explained, the length of life for humans is not certain. This is because it is the characteristic of our dimension that karma can ripen very easily and quickly. That is why Buddha called our dimension of Jambudvipa[10] the field of karma. So, while all humans have the suffering that comes with birth, old age, illness, and death, some live longer and some shorter, depending on their karma.

The *asuras* have much longer lives than humans, and the *devas* have much longer lives than them, many thousands of years at least. There are many kinds of *devas* with different conditions and different lifespans. But their condition is always connected to their karma, and karma is always connected to time. So even though *devas* can have unlimited enjoyments for thousands of years, eventually they die and fall into lower realms. In the end, all sentient beings die and are reborn in different conditions.

།ལོ་དང་ཟླ་བ་ཞག་དང་དུས་ཚོགས་དང་།
།སྐད་ཅིག་མི་རྟག་འཇིག་ཅིང་གཡོ་བ་སྟེ།
།དུས་བཞི་འགྱུར་བས་རྣམ་པར་སྐྱོ་བ་ཅན།
།རང་གི་ཚེ་ཡང་མི་རྟག་འགྱུར་བ་སོམས།

Years, months, days, hours, and single moments
Are impermanent – they vanish, and [time] moves on.

---

10 In traditional Buddhist cosmology, our world of Jambudvipa is one of four major continents surrounding Mount Meru. See Jamgön Kongtrul Lodrö Thaye, *Myriad Worlds.*

Because they change, the four seasons have the nature
of sorrow and grief.
Consider how your own life is just as impermanent
and changing.

We can understand impermanence just by observing how the four seasons pass in the course of one year. First there is springtime, and everything seems very nice: all of nature is breathing, growing, and becoming green. After three months it is summertime, and then all the flowers open and look beautiful. In our human condition, we can say that young people are like flowers in the summertime: they are active and happy, they may become famous, and so on. But flowers and green leaves do not remain forever. After a while autumn arrives, the weather changes, and the leaves begin to fall from the trees. In the same way, whatever you might have been doing with your life or whatever you wanted to do, your possibilities lessen as you become old. Finally wintertime comes: everything dies, and then the cycle repeats itself.

Look at a clock for a while and watch how its hands are always moving ahead, never backward. Our breathing is just like this: if you consider that in your life you will have one million breaths, for example, and then you take one breath, now you no longer have one million breaths left. Of course, as we go ahead in our lives, this number is always diminishing, breath by breath, until it goes down to nothing and our life is finished.

།ཡིད་བརྟན་མེད་དོ་ལུས་སྲོག་འབྲལ་དུ་ཉེ།
།སང་དང་བདག་གི་ཚེ་ཟད་དུས་འདི་གཉིས།
།སྔོན་ལ་གང་འབྱུང་ངེས་པ་མེད་དོ་ཞེས།
།དེ་རིང་ཉིད་ནས་ངེས་པར་བསམ་པར་བྱ།

So from this moment on, think without fail,
"There is no security! My body and life will soon be parted
And I cannot even know which will come first:
Tomorrow or the end of my life."

Being alive means that your life energy is connected to your body. Your present life continues until your life energy and your body separate, at which point you die. We generally hope or expect to live for eighty or ninety years. Some people go to an astrologer and when the astrologer says, "You will live seventy-five years," they think this is how long their life will be. But here Longchenpa says we cannot even know what will come first: tomorrow or our next life. In fact, what he says is true, there really is no guarantee.

It is not sufficient to learn and think about it intellectually, because being aware of impermanence does not mean just sitting and thinking about our death for hours. Instead, it means we keep this awareness throughout our daily life and allow it to affect our behavior. Being aware of impermanence is particularly important for practitioners, because it makes us think about the fact that we have received such important teachings, such important practices, and then we understand that we should do these practices now, because otherwise we may not have another chance.

This awareness will also help us have more respect for others, because even if we have some problems with them, these problems will not seem so important. For example, maybe you want to confront someone or argue with them, but if you have this awareness of impermanence you will understand that there is no need because tomorrow none of you may even exist. Or, for example, you may feel tired of being with your husband or wife, and want to separate, saying, "It's so difficult being together for even one day or one week, so how can we remain together like this for the rest of our lives?" In this moment you are thinking that the "rest of your life" means many years, but it actually could be finished this very evening.

When I was growing up in Tibet, young people would sometimes come from the countryside to my family's home to help us harvest our crops. My mother was always very kind to them and would provide lots of food and wine for them to enjoy. I remember one evening, many of these young people were sitting around together, eating and drinking, singing, dancing, and enjoying themselves until very late at night. Then some of them went to sleep in the fields, because at that time of year it was not so cold in my region. But the next morning when we woke up, we found that one young girl had died during the night. Nobody knew how or why it happened: in the evening she had been dancing and singing with everybody else, and she seemed very happy. When we say there is no guarantee when we will die, I always remember this girl.

A long time ago in Tibet there was an important teacher named Atisha[11] who had some exceptional students. In his teachings, he mainly emphasized Sutrayana principles, and taught that the most important practice to do in one's lifetime was to be aware of impermanence. For example, when they went to bed in the evening, Atisha's followers would prepare everything just as if they were preparing to die: they would turn their cups over and not prepare for breakfast, they would let the embers in their fireplace go out, and so on, because they knew that they might not wake up the next morning.

There is a famous story about this. Once there was a practitioner who lived in a cave, and outside this cave was a small thornbush. Every time he went to collect water, he would pass this bush and it would rip his clothes. So of course he thought of cutting the bush down. But every time this thought occurred to him, his awareness of impermanence

11 Atisha Dipankara Shrijnana, 980–1054.

would arise, and he would think, "Since I don't know if I will be alive tomorrow or not, there is no need. I should use the time to practice instead." He continued like this day after day, and the bush grew bigger and bigger, but he never cut it down. This is an example of really living with the awareness of impermanence.

།འཆི་བ་བས་ཀྱང་སྐྱེ་བའི་སྡུག་བསྔལ་འཇིགས།
།གང་དུ་སྐྱེས་ཀྱང་བདེ་བ་འགའ་མེད་དེ།
།འཁོར་བའི་རང་བཞིན་མེ་ཡི་འོབས་ལྟ་བུ།
།འདི་ལས་ད་རེས་ཐར་ཐབས་བཙལ་བར་བྱ།

The suffering of birth is even more terrifying than death –
There is no joy at all wherever you are born.
By its very nature, samsara is like a pit of flames,
So this time you must seek a way to free yourself from it.

Now we have the third mindfulness: the function of karma and its relation to our cycle of transmigration in samsara.

We know that we exist in time, and that time is always moving ahead. But we should also understand that while time is going by, we never remain passive, without thinking or acting. Our mind is like a monkey: a monkey never stops, it is always doing something. In the same way, our mind is constantly creating different kinds of thoughts, emotions, fantasies, and all kinds of confusion. Then, acting on these emotions and fantasies, we create so many problems. When our actions are connected to our emotions, we produce negative karma; this is happening constantly, which means we are constantly accumulating causes for existence in the six realms of samsara.

Samsara arises because of dualistic vision. When we are in a state of dualistic vision we always experience attachment and anger, accepting some phenomena and rejecting others. Throughout our lives these are our two most dominant emotions; they are just like two legs that we use to move around in samsara. When we walk, we put forward our right leg, then our left leg, right, left, right, left. In the same way, as we go through our life we have attachment, anger, attachment, anger. This is how we are always going ahead in samsara.

Although these emotions of attachment and anger are not at all necessary, our habit of being conditioned by them is very strong. For example, if you go to a garden to enjoy the flowers, your intention is not to judge which flowers are better than others, but because of this habit you find yourself thinking, "I like this flower very much." If you like one flower very much, it means that you do not like the other flowers as much as this one, and that means you have started accepting and rejecting. This is our habit – we never remain neutral – and in this way we are always accumulating karma.

Many people think Westerners have no knowledge of karma, but this is not true. It is just that Westerners generally do not use the word "karma." For example, in many Western films and books, if a person does something negative, things eventually go badly for them. And if someone in the story does something very good, even if at that moment he is suffering or has to make some sacrifices, eventually things end well for him. This shows an understanding of the principle of karma. At the very least, we all know that if we eat something bad tonight, we will have pain in our stomach tomorrow, because just living in our dimension requires this kind of awareness about cause and effect. This, in fact, is the principle of karma, so we cannot say that Westerners lack such understanding.

We can also understand how karma is related to the principle of reincarnation, of transmigration in samsara. This involves going a little deeper in our understanding. For example, Buddha said that if we want to know what we did in our past lives, we should observe our present condition: if you have a good physical body and few difficulties or problems, this is the fruit of your actions in your past life. On the other hand, some people encounter problems even from the time they are born, and this is also the product of karma from their previous life.

Even when two people are born into the same family with the same parents and the same upbringing, as they grow older they become more and more different from each other. Different circumstances manifest in their lives, and they have contact with different kinds of people. All of these things are also related to their karma from previous lives. So we can understand what we did before by observing our present conditions.

Then Buddha said that if we want to know how our future will be, we should observe our present actions. In fact, everything we do in our life creates good or bad karma, and this is why we must really try to perform only good actions, cultivate good karma as much as possible, and avoid creating bad karma so that we will not have to experience heavy suffering in the future.

If you want to have a more precise understanding of how we accumulate karma, it is important to be aware of the three conditions necessary to produce a seed of karma. First, you must have the intention to do something. Second, you must go ahead and do it, either by yourself or by asking someone else to do it for you. In either case, the action is committed in accordance with your intention. Finally, when the action has been successfully accomplished, you must feel satisfied. As soon as all three conditions are present, you have produced a seed of karma.

What if, on the other hand, you have a negative intention but do not act on it, or you do act on it but afterward you feel regret? In these cases you would still accumulate negative karma, but instead of becoming a seed of karma with the full potential to manifest a result in the future, it only becomes a kind of obstacle, blocking positive conditions from manifesting in your life, or preventing you from increasing your clarity or attaining realization. This is also true if you do something accidentally, like stepping on an insect: it is not the same as the karma of killing that insect intentionally, but it does create a small obstacle for you.

There is another point that is important to understand. Some people have the idea that accumulating karma is like having a debt that has to be repaid, or committing themselves to doing something they will then be powerless to avoid. For example, if they contract an illness they might think, "What can I do? This is my life, this is my karma." That is not a correct understanding of how karma works at all. There must always be a primary cause or karmic seed from the past, but how that seed matures and ripens is related to our present situation. So if we are aware, it is always possible for us to change our situation in order to change how our karma will manifest.

In fact, we have infinite seeds of various kinds of negative karma, but not all of these seeds are maturing and manifesting their results at the same moment or in the same way, because they only manifest in a particular way due to certain secondary causes. A poisonous seed needs earth, water, light, and so on if it is to grow into a dangerous plant. In the same way, in our own condition, when all the necessary secondary causes are present, a karmic seed will manifest in a way that corresponds to those secondary causes, and it is then that we will experience the result of our karma. So even if we carelessly plant a poisonous seed in the earth, we can become aware and notice when it begins to grow into a plant; we can notice that a seed of negative karma is beginning to mature. Then we can try to determine which secondary causes are allowing this to happen, and we can remove those causes. In this case, we can at least change or lessen the heaviness of how our karma manifests. This is how it is possible to prevent a seed of karma from fully ripening.

Of course, the best thing for us to do is try to avoid committing negative actions in the first place. So if we know these things but continue to commit negative actions, we need the fourth mindfulness, which is related to the infinite kinds of suffering we experience in the realms of samsara.

In our condition of samsara, everything is suffering: death and birth both have the nature of suffering, and any dimension of the six realms into which we take rebirth will always be a continuation of that suffering; not a single realm exists where we can find only joy and happiness. The nature of samsara is like a dimension of fire. In a dimension of fire there is absolutely no way to find any comfort. So we should try to free ourselves now, while we have this good opportunity. It is extremely important that we free ourselves.

།དམྱལ་བ་ཚ་གྲང་ཡི་དྭགས་བཀྲེས་དང་སྐོམ།
།དུད་འགྲོ་གཅིག་ཟ་གླེན་རྨོངས་སྡུག་བསྔལ་ཏེ།
།མི་རྣམས་ཉེས་གསུམ་བརྒྱད་ཀྱིས་ཡོངས་སུ་གདུང་།
།ལྷ་མིན་འཐབ་རྩོད་ལྷ་རྣམས་འཆི་འཕོ་ལྟུང་།

Hell beings are afflicted by heat and cold, *pretas* by hunger
and thirst,
Animals by being eaten and by the daze of stupidity.
Humans are tormented by the three faults
and eight [conditions],
Asuras by fighting and struggle, *devas* by death and downfall.

Here Longchenpa explains in just a few words the various kinds of suffering that beings experience in samsara. All these kinds of suffering are produced by our karma. As we are distracted and influenced by our emotions day after day, we accumulate great amounts of negative karma, which then manifest as suffering. For example, the karma we accumulate through anger can produce the dimensions of hell. This does not happen by getting angry just two or three times. Some people are angry many times every day, and as they continue accumulating this karma of anger year after year, life after life, they will eventually have a sufficient cause for being born in a hell realm where they will experience the suffering of heat or cold. Generally, we say there are eight hot hells and eight cold hells, and also what are called day-long hells and neighboring hells. In the day-long hells you live for one day and then die, but are then forced to repeat this over and over again. The neighboring hells are mainly a consequence of having very strong attachment. In this kind of dimension, you find yourself in a desert where there is a small hill with some dry trees, and from the top of this hill a person you love is calling for you. But when you approach this hill the situation changes: a strong wind arises, and the branches of the trees become knives that cut you into thousands of pieces. Then you die, but just as in the day-long hells, this happens over and over again, an infinite number of times.

The karma of attachment can also lead to rebirth as a *preta.* As human beings it is normal for us to have strong attachment, such as attachment to our wealth and property, to other people, and so on. But eventually, if we accumulate enough karma linked to this kind of attachment, it can become the cause of our rebirth in a *preta* realm, where there is nothing to eat or drink, or where any food that does exist manifests as filth or as fire. In general, we call *pretas* hungry ghosts because they are always hungry and because they are a bit like beings in the *bardo* (the intermediate state between death and rebirth), who have what we call a mental body, even though due to their karma *pretas'* bodies are more substantial. So they are always hungry and thirsty but can never find food or drink, and even if they do find something, when they try put it in their mouth it changes into something else, like fire.

There is a famous story about this. Once a bodhisattva came across an arhat[12] sitting in a chair to which a *preta* was tied with a cord. The arhat asked the bodhisattva, "Could you stay here for a while and look after this *preta* so that I can go and do something?" The bodhisattva agreed, so the arhat went away, leaving him alone with the *preta*. He could see that this *preta* was very miserable, very hungry. Then he noticed that there was some food right in front of the *preta*, but he could not reach it because he was tied up. The *preta* looked up and said to the bodhisattva, "Please give me a little food, I am very hungry." Of course, the bodhisattva felt compassion, so he gave him some of the food. But as soon as the *preta* put the food in his mouth it turned to fire, and many parts of his body began to burn. After a while, the arhat returned, and when he saw the *preta* he said, "Why did you give this *preta* food? *Pretas* have no cause for enjoying food." The bodhisattva said, "I gave it to him because of my practice of compassion." To this, the arhat said, "Do not think that I have no compassion! It is just that it is not possible for *pretas* to eat food." So you can see what the condition of *pretas* is like.

Then we have the realm of animals. Beings take rebirth as animals through the karma of dullness and ignorance: as animals they have no capacity to learn or to develop knowledge as humans can, so they only perpetuate their ignorance. Their other great suffering is that they are always being eaten by each other. Big animals eat small ones, small animals eat still smaller ones. Of all sentient beings, the karmic vision of animals is the closest to that of humans, and animals also have the

12 Literally "foe destroyer." This state is the goal of the Hinayana path of individual liberation.

same physical aspect as humans, so for this reason we can directly see many kinds of animals.

There are also many animals we cannot see, and even some that do not correspond to our logic. For example, we believe that fire can eliminate any physical substance, that if you burn something all that will remain is ash. But there are some animals who live in fire and are not burned by it; these beings are nothing like spirits or *devas,* but are simply animals whose condition does not correspond to our logic. So many kinds of beings exist that are considered to be animals, but what they have in common is that they produce their dimension of karmic vision through the karma of ignorance.

These three – hell beings, *pretas,* and animals – are what we call the lower states of existence. Why are they called that? Because they generally have no opportunity to follow the teachings, so it is impossible for them to practice and attain realization.

Even in that kind of state, sometimes, in some exceptional situations, a being can become liberated. For example, if someone has a special connection with an enlightened being and is then born as a hell being or *preta,* the enlightened being can manifest in their dimension and help them become liberated from that state. But this is not the way things usually go for these classes of beings. In general, it is impossible to do anything in these states but suffer and accumulate more karma. This is why we call them the lower realms.

Then we have the three higher states: those of human beings, *asuras,* and the different classes of *devas.* In some teachings, we hear that the cause for human birth is linked to pride. In fact, our human condition does seem very much connected to pride: as humans, we tend to have strong egos. For example, we always think we are better and know better than others. When we discuss something with another person, we always think what we say is the truth. In fact, we may be wrong, but still we argue for hours and hours, insisting that we are right. Our ego not only affects our ordinary life but also our approach to the Dharma. For example, we can become very intellectual and then think that our knowledge, what we have understood, is perfect. This is only our ego.

Also, if some problem or tension arises between ourselves and another person or group of people, we can think, "Everything I have done is perfect. They are the ones at fault." In this way we search for somebody to blame, trying to discover who is the guilty one, but we never look at ourselves. Buddha taught in the sutras that everything is interdependent. If this is true, it means that the problems we have with others, too, arise through interdependence. If we are totally innocent, there is no way for a problem to ever arise between ourselves and anybody else. If we understand this, then whenever we have a problem, our first step should be to look for the root of the problem within ourselves. But because of our ego and our pride, we never seem to do things this way. So you can see how pride can dominate our lives.

Alternately, some Dzogchen tantras explain that the cause of human birth is the combined force of the karma of all five emotions in equal proportion.[13] We can understand this point of view by observing how a strong mixture of all these emotions is constantly manifesting in our lives. Also, whenever we do any kind of purification practice, we obtain much more benefit if we try to purify all negative emotions equally, instead of focusing on pride alone.

In any case, here Longchenpa explains that as human beings we experience the suffering of always being conditioned by the three poisons and distracted by the eight worldly conditions.

Then there are the *asuras*. *Asuras* almost seem like a kind of *deva*: they have much more power and capability than humans, and they

13 The five poisons are ignorance, attachment, anger, jealousy, and pride.

also live much more comfortably than we do. But the cause of taking birth as an *asura* is jealousy, the emotion that dominates *asuras.* So even though many possibilities for happiness exist in their dimension and their lifespan is very long, they never have any peace. Their jealousy drives them to continuously accumulate negative karma. Whenever they have contact with *devas* and see that the *devas* are superior to them, they feel incredibly jealous. This jealousy drives them to dedicate all their effort to making war with the *devas,* but of course the *devas* always win.

As humans, we also experience jealousy when the secondary causes manifest, but not like the *asuras,* who are really overwhelmed by jealousy at all times. So this is the suffering of the *asuras.*

Finally there are the *devas.* Just as with humans, some sources say the cause of taking birth as a *deva* is pride and some say the cause is a combination of all the emotions. In any case, as we explained already, the lives of *devas* are free of problems and full of enjoyment, and they live for a very long time, much longer than *asuras. Devas* do not have the kinds of problems we face as humans: they have a miraculous, painless birth, they do not grow old, and they are never afflicted by illness. So from birth onward they have nothing but pleasure and enjoyment.

The real situation, however, is that by manifesting the enjoyments of their dimension, they are using up the enormous amounts of positive karma they accumulated in previous lives. They do this until all their positive karma is consumed, at which point they receive a kind of indication that they will die after one week. Now they know they are facing a big problem. Not only will they die, but with their mental clarity they can see that as a result of having exhausted all their positive karma they will not take rebirth as a human or animal, but will fall directly into hell.

So *devas* might live for many thousands of years or more without having any problems at all, but they spend the end of their lives in a state of extreme suffering. Various dimensions of *devas* exists, and you can learn about them, but it is not really important to know all the details. It is more important to know the general condition of these six realms of samsara, and to understand that happiness cannot be found in any of them.

You must not consider that these six realms have anything like a geographical location. If you search for the actual locations of the hell or *preta* dimensions, you will not find them anywhere, because they are not anything concrete that we can perceive from within our human condition, with our human karmic vision. But we should not think this means they do not exist. All sentient beings have their condition, their dimension, and the way these dimensions manifest depends on our karma. Now we are human beings, and all human beings share the same karmic vision of the human dimension. But in the same way, all beings in the hell realms share the same karmic vision and they all perceive hell.

So according to the Dzogchen teachings, nothing concrete exists at all, not one of these dimensions: just as Buddha said, everything is unreal. The only cause for us to experience these realms is the ripening of our karma. For example, if it were possible for one being from each of the six realms to meet on the bank of the same river, what would they see? The human would see water for drinking or bathing. Certain animals would perceive it as a home. A *preta* does not have the karmic cause to see water, so the river would appear to him as blood, pus, and rotten things, or even if he were able to see it as water and tried to drink some, as soon as it entered his mouth it would become fire. On the other hand, a *deva* standing by the same river would see it as pure nectar, and an *asura* would see it as weapons with which to fight the *devas*. So everything we perceive is manifested by our karmic potential. Since nothing has a concrete existence, we cannot say that the perceptions of any one of these different kinds of beings are more real or accurate than those of any other.

The purpose of these explanations of the six realms is to give an idea of the kinds of suffering we can experience as a result of our karma, but we must understand that the particular details with which Buddha explained these realms are connected to history, to ancient Indian culture and knowledge. Some people who are extremely traditional followers of Buddhism still believe that the world is flat and that in the center is Mount Meru surrounded by four continents. Because this is the description of the universe found in the *Abhidharmakosha,*[14] these people believe that it must be the "Buddhist" way of seeing things, and that this Buddhist way of seeing things is really true. But if Buddha said everything is unreal, how can Mount Meru be real? The *Kalachakra Tantra* is also a Buddhist teaching, but its explanation of Mount Meru and all the continents does not correspond at all with the explanation found in the *Abhidharmakosha.* Even the explanation of our universe in the Mahayana sutras is completely different from what Buddha explained to his Hinayana followers.

In all these cases, Buddha was explaining things according to the way people in a particular time and place already saw the world. There is nothing ultimately real or important about these things, but Buddha used them as a basis to communicate knowledge and understanding about something more important, like the fact that all these relative things are actually unreal. I am one hundred percent sure that if Buddha were teaching here today, he would say the world is round, not because that is something real, but because this is how we now perceive

---

14 An important text in the Hinayana system. See Jamgön Kongtrul Lodrö Thaye, *Myriad Worlds,* for a discussion of Abhidharma, Kalachakra, and Dzogchen cosmology.

it. Buddha knows very well that a round world is also unreal, but since the relative level is not the main point, he can speak of a round world as a kind of example, to communicate with his students in a way they will understand.

We should keep this in mind when we learn about the different categories of hell realms or the various kinds of *pretas, devas,* and so on. This does not mean we should not learn about such things, but we should remember that the main point is to understand how the potentiality of karma that we accumulate through our various emotions creates these different kinds of suffering.

།བདེ་སྡུག་འགྱུར་ཞིང་འདུ་བྱེད་སྡུག་བསྔལ་མང་།
།ལྷ་ཡུལ་འབྱོར་བདེ་དག་ལས་ཆེ་འཕོས་ནས་།
།སླར་ཡང་དམྱལ་བའི་མེ་ནང་འཇུག་འཚལ་བས།
།འདི་འདྲ་བསམས་ནས་སྲིད་ལས་འདའ་བར་མཛོད།

Pleasure changes into pain, and myriad sufferings arise
through being conditioned.
Passing away from the celestial realms of abundance,
joy, and purity,
We are forced again to enter into the flames of hell.
Reflect on how it really is like this, and leave samsara.

Sometimes we might feel slight happiness, but even that can easily transform into suffering. To understand this, we only have to look at the situation of the *devas*: they enjoy everything for a long time, but once their merit has been consumed, they fall into hell. So, understanding that we can never attain real happiness in any of these karmic dimensions, we must completely free ourselves from the dualistic karmic vision that is the root of it all.

Most of the time we are distracted and ignorant of our real situation, just thinking there are some nice things to do, see, or experience. Of course, we can enjoy some of these nice things if we maintain our awareness and do not fall into dualistic vision. But if we maintain dualistic vision, our enjoyments will just become causes for accumulating negative karma and perpetuating samsara. In this respect we are like insects flying into a fire at night: attracted by the light, they want to go there, but then they burn up and die, so all they experience is suffering. In the same way, we might get some enjoyment from relating to the objects of our senses, but in general our way of relating to these pleasures only creates problems for us.

For example, if two young people are in love but their parents do not approve of their relationship, they may decide to run away together. But then, if they do not succeed in escaping, they might decide that rather than be separated they should die together. So we can see how this situation begins with enjoyment, with two people being in love, and then becomes the cause of suffering, not happiness. These kinds of things happen all the time. So knowing that this is the real situation, we must decide to liberate ourselves from samsara.

Abandoning Worldly Goals

།ཚེ་འདིའི་སྣང་བ་རྨི་ལམ་སད་ཀ་འདྲ།
།འགྱུར་ཞིང་མི་རྟག་དོར་ནས་འགྲོ་དགོས་པས།
།འཁོར་དང་ལོངས་སྤྱོད་ལ་སོགས་ཅི་ཞིག་བྱ།
།ད་ལྟ་ཉིད་དུ་ཆོས་ལ་འབད་པར་བགྱི།

The appearances of this life are like those of a dream
just as you are waking:
Shifting and transient, you must leave them behind and go.

Of what use, then, are companions, possessions, and the rest?
From this very moment on, apply yourself to the Dharma.

Our karmic vision in this life is like a dream. As soon as we awaken from a dream we discover that it was all unreal. In the same way, even if we have had some happiness in our lifetime, with many friends and people who depend on us, and even if we have had power, fame, and success in business, all these things are relative and impermanent, just like a dream, and none of them will be of any use when we die. We will have to leave them all behind and go away without them. So we should understand that this is our situation, and instead of giving too much importance to these kinds of things, we should dedicate our lives to the practice of Dharma.

།འདོད་པ་དུག་དང་མཚོན་དང་མེ་འདྲ་ཞིང་།
།ཡོངས་སུ་གདུངས་བས་བདེ་བའི་གོ་སྐབས་མེད།
།བསགས་དང་བསྲུང་དང་སྤེལ་བས་སྡུག་བསྔལ་ཞིང་།
།ཁེངས་དང་འཛུངས་དང་སེར་སྣས་རྟག་ཏུ་འཆིང་།

Desire is like a poison, a weapon, or fire:
It overwhelms you with pain, leaving no chance for joy.
Suffering as you amass, protect, and increase,
You are forever shackled by arrogance, possessiveness,
and greed.

Being distracted by our desire always produces suffering. It is like a deadly poison, and it can destroy things just like a knife, a gun, or an army. It is like a fire that burns everything it touches. When we have strong desire, even if at first it feels like we are pursuing happiness, our desire never leads us to the happiness we seek.

We have to be aware of the fact that when we accumulate money, precious things, and so on, and then make sacrifices to protect what we have and multiply these riches, what we are really doing day after day is acquiring, protecting, and increasing our own suffering. As Paltrul Rinpoche said, "If we have a goat we have goat problems; if we have a horse we have horse problems." However many things we have, we have that many problems. If we do not understand this, we will always feel that we need more wealth and possessions; we will never feel satisfied, but will think that we feel this way because we have not yet accumulated enough things.

For example, if you begin with nothing and then buy a bicycle, this might make you feel happy for a while. But as soon as you have the opportunity to buy a car, you will be unhappy with your bicycle and feel you need a car. Then, as soon as you have the chance to buy a bigger or better car, you will feel that this is what you need to do. Or you might build a small house and feel happy for a while, but eventually you will want a bigger house, and when you are still not satisfied with a bigger house, you might decide you really need two houses.

This is our condition. All of us have this kind of desire, and whenever we allow ourselves to be distracted and conditioned by it, it does nothing but increase our suffering and our problems.

།ཀུན་དང་རྩོད་བཅས་ཉོན་མོངས་ཟག་པ་འཕེལ།
།འདུ་འཛིན་གཡེང་ཞིང་ལུས་དང་སྲོག་ལ་རྦོལ།
།དོན་དང་བྱ་བ་མང་ཞིང་ཚོས་དང་འགལ།
།འཕགས་པ་རྣམས་ཀྱིས་རྟག་ཏུ་སྨད་པ་ཡིན།

In conflict with everyone, the emotions
that defile you increase;
Caught up in worldly endeavors, you risk your body and life.

With many projects and things to do, you contradict
the Dharma
And are always reproached by the Noble Ones.

As we struggle to satisfy our desires we also create problems for other people by constantly arguing and fighting with them. When we behave in this way, many different emotions arise and multiply while at the same time we become increasingly attached to our desires. The more we fight for what we desire, the more real, important, and worth fighting for they seem to be.

When we are conditioned by strong desires, we always have many things to do, so we are always occupied with these tasks and never feel free. Of course, we also feel that we never have time for practice. This situation can become very heavy, and while we are struggling to accumulate possessions or gain power and position, we can even destroy our life and lose our precious human body.

Since none of this corresponds to the real sense of the Dharma, holy beings who hold real knowledge will consider that all this is negative, that our ideas are not good, and that we are really not doing a good job with our life.

།འདོད་པ་ཆུང་རྣམས་རང་གིས་དགེ་བ་འཕེལ།
།དེས་ན་ཞི་བའི་ཐར་ལམ་ཞུགས་རྣམས་ཀྱིས།
།འདོད་པ་ཆུང་ཞིང་ཆོག་ཤེས་ལྡན་པར་མཛོད།
།འདོད་པ་ཟད་ན་འཕགས་པ་དངོས་ཡིན་ལ།
།འདོད་པ་ཆུང་ན་འཕགས་པའི་རིགས་ཞེས་བྱ།

For those with little desire, virtues naturally increase,
So those who enter the path to the peace of liberation
Should decrease desire and cultivate contentment.

When desire has been extinguished, you are an actual Noble One;
If you have little desire, you are said to be in the family
of the Noble Ones.

So we can see that whenever we let ourselves be conditioned by our desires, heavy emotions and suffering increase. On the other hand, when we lessen our desires we can be happy with very little and, living in this way, our good karma and merit will automatically increase. For this reason, Longchenpa says here that people who enter the path of Dharma should try to reduce their desires as much as possible.

Desire is always related to our sense of attachment. For example, some people try to accumulate money even as they are dying, despite the fact that, when they die, they cannot take even one dollar with them. Such a person may think, "I want to accumulate wealth and possessions now so I can leave them to my family." But in the process of accumulating these things, he may commit many negative actions and, unlike money and possessions, when he dies, this negative karma does go with him. So it is important to be satisfied with a simple life. You should not feel that you need a big house or a great amount of food. Of course, if you feel hungry and have no food, you will have the desire to eat, and that is fine because eating is necessary in our human condition. But then, once you have a little food, you should stop there and feel satisfied.

We can understand this principle very well by considering how Buddhist monks in ancient times, including Buddha himself, did things. To keep his monks from developing desire, Buddha made a rule that they could not keep or store food. Instead, every day they had to go into town with their bowls, to the doorstep of four or five families, and collect a small amount of food for that day. Then, before midday, they would return to the forest to sit and eat together. They would not eat again until the next day. All of this was for the sake of decreasing desire.

This way of doing things is especially characteristic of the Hinayana approach. Although this approach is not necessary for followers of the Mahayana, we must still know the basic principle behind it, and must always try to apply it and decrease our desire. The Mahayana training is not based on rules and vows, but on observing ourselves and our intention. So, for example, if you notice that you are thinking, "It is good that I have this, but maybe I need something more," you can immediately recognize that this thought is based on desire, and think instead, "No, what I have now is enough." When we conduct ourselves in this way, our desire decreases and we become more content, and when we become content our virtues automatically increase.

Longchenpa explains here that if you have no desire at all, you have become a real bodhisattva, and if you have only a small amount of desire you are close to being a bodhisattva, or are in the family of the bodhisattvas.

།འདོད་ལྡན་སྡུག་བསྔལ་ཉོན་མོངས་འཕེལ་བ་ལྟར།
།འདོད་པ་ཆུང་རྣམས་ངང་གིས་དགེ་བ་འཕེལ།
།དེ་བས་སྔོན་གྱི་དམ་པའི་རྗེས་འགྲོ་བས།
།རྟག་ཏུ་ཆོག་ཤེས་ཡོ་བྱད་བསྡུང་བར་བྱ།

Just as sufferings and emotions grow for those
who have desire,
For those with little desire,
virtues spontaneously increase.
So to follow in the footsteps of the holy beings of the past,
Be content at all times and reduce your possessions.

In brief, if you have strong desires you will find that your emotions and suffering multiply easily, but if you decrease your desires, it is merit and virtue that multiply and develop. So we try to behave in the same way as the holy masters, great bodhisattvas, and realized beings of ancient times: we must learn to be easily satisfied, living in a simple way with few possessions. In particular, people who are training primarily in the Sutrayana way should try to live like this.

།མི་དང་འགྲོགས་པའི་ཉེས་བའང་ཚད་མེད་དེ།
།དོན་མེད་རྣམ་པར་གཡེངས་ཤིང་བྱ་བའང་མང་།
།ཁྲོ་དང་འཐབ་རྩོད་འཕེལ་ཞིང་ཆགས་སྡང་སྐྱེ།
།རྟག་ཏུ་སྡུག་བསྔལ་འགོ་ཞིང་སྙིང་པོ་མེད།

Keeping close ties with others brings inestimable harm:
You are totally and meaninglessly distracted,
and have many things to do;
Hostilities and strife proliferate, attachment
and hatred emerge.
You are constantly infected by these sufferings,
and this is pointless.

If we stay together with good practitioners, of course we will benefit, because we will be surrounded by positive influences and good role models to follow. But if we maintain close connections with ordinary people, we cannot really be sure how it will turn out, because we can never really know who these people are inside, or what their real condition is.

When we are involved with such people, we can easily get caught up in all kinds of activities that are of no benefit at all, and this can become a very heavy situation, particularly when we become easily agitated and start to fight and struggle with people. Sometimes people quickly become good friends, but after a few months they are no longer friends, and may even think of each other as enemies. This is our human condition. Just as circumstances are always changing, so are people, and with these changes our emotions of attachment and anger only develop further and further and become heavier and heavier. As we know, our ego mainly manifests itself through thoughts of: "I like it; I dislike it. I accept it; I reject it." We are constantly thinking in this way, and can go through our whole life like this, but there is nothing positive or meaningful in doing so. The only function of this way of living is to produce suffering.

།ཇི་ལྟར་བྱས་ཀྱང་མགུ་བའི་དུས་མེད་ལ།
།གང་ལྟར་བསྟན་ཀྱང་ཕན་པའི་གོ་སྐབས་དཀའ།
།དེ་ལྟར་མཉན་ཡང་ལེགས་པའི་ཆོས་མེད་ལ།
།བཤེས་ལྟར་མཐུན་ཡང་ཐ་མ་འབྲལ་བར་འགྱུར།

Whatever you have done, they will never be satisfied.
However you try to teach them, the chances of benefit are slim.
Even when they do listen, they lack the excellent qualities
    [to understand].
And however harmoniously you relate to them,
    you will separate in the end.

We know very well that even if we always do our best for other people, they are never satisfied. When they criticize us instead of thanking us for our help, we feel angry and offended, and if we discuss the situation we may end up arguing and fighting with them instead of helping them. But if you are a practitioner, you can approach this situation differently. Remember that even Buddha could not satisfy everyone. This is just how it is. If you are doing something of benefit and you are sure that it is really appropriate to the circumstances and is helping people, you can just feel happy about this and go ahead with your activities, and not pay any attention to their criticism.

For example, if I am doing my best to benefit others, trying to do service for a group of people or community, some people are happy but some are angry and criticize me. But I really do not care, because I know from the teachings that this is just the condition of samsaric beings. I only feel a little sad for these people, because this kind of behavior is a manifestation of ignorance and ego, which only causes more suffering for them. I always try to help people like this to understand the teachings so they can see how their egos are manifesting. But if, day after day, year after year, they do not change at all, then I really feel sad.

So you see, even if you are teaching and explaining the Dharma correctly, some people may understand what you are teaching, but not everybody can enjoy that benefit. Even if we try to make people understand the most essential teachings of Dzogchen – how to integrate everything in the state of Guruyoga[15] – some will be happy, but others will not understand that this is the real essence of the teachings, the most important thing. They may say, "This is boring. There is a very famous teaching called such-and-such. Please teach me that!" Then, no matter how many times you explain, they never understand the real sense of the Dharma.

Also, when something happens, even people who have become close friends and are always careful to be kind to each other may

15 The practice of Guruyoga, the essence of the practice of Dzogchen. Discussed in depth in the commentary on the section on following a qualified teacher (Second Dharma). See index for other mentions.

manifest many differences, stop liking each other, and part ways. This can even happen between children and their parents, between brothers and sisters, and so on. People separate from each other like this all the time.

So when we have these kinds of close connections – with many people depending on us in different ways, many kinds of relationships, friendships, and so on – even if we try to do our best for them and to make them happy, in the end everything is impermanent and these connections may just become secondary causes for negativity and obstacles to progress in our practice.

།དེ་བས་འཁོར་དང་མཛའ་བཤེས་གཉེན་འདུན་ལ།
།ཉེ་བར་བརྟེན་པའི་འབྲེལ་འདྲིས་ཀུན་སྤང་སྟེ།
།གཅིག་པུར་དབེན་པར་དམ་ཆོས་སྒྲུབ་པའི་ཕྱིར།
།དེ་རིང་ཉིད་ནས་ངེས་པར་འབད་པར་བྱ།

So abandon all relationships of mutual dependence
With followers, close friends, and family,
And from this day forward sincerely strive
To accomplish the sacred Dharma in solitude.

For these reasons, Longchenpa advises us that, instead of maintaining ordinary relationships with these kinds of people, it is better to go away and stay alone somewhere quiet, and just do our practice so that we can have total realization. This is what Longchenpa did. When he was young, he lived in many monasteries and other places, and also travelled around giving teachings. People called him Samyepa, the Teacher of Samye, because he lived and taught for a long time at Samye Monastery, which was built by Guru Padmasambhava in central Tibet. But later he began to see things differently, and decided to go away and live alone on a mountain called Kangri Thökar.[16] He spent many years there doing practice. So he is saying here that this is how we can benefit others more.

Many practitioners decide to go this way because they consider that giving many teachings and having many students is a little negative, that it can be a kind of obstacle to their realization. Of course, there is nothing negative about having ten students who are dedicated and whose behavior is perfect. If someone like Longchenpa or Milarepa is living on a mountain and a student comes who is seriously interested in receiving teachings from him, this student needs to be ready to make some sacrifices, because it is not easy to follow such a teacher. So this indicates that the student is seriously interested. But not many students are like this.

For example, my uncle Khyentse Rinpoche lived in a cave, in a place where there was always snow, even in the summertime. In that area there was no other place for people to stay. But once, he gave a very essential teaching called the Nyingthig Yazhi,[17] and many students came from different places. Nearly forty people came, but in his cave had space for only twenty people to sit in the usual way, so we were all sitting with our knees up against our chests. Every day when he finished teaching, all of the students had to go down the mountain, because there were some trees below where they could take shelter for the night. In the morning, they walked back up the mountain to his cave. Of course, when people have the capacity to make sacrifices like this in order to receive teachings, they become good students.

---

16 "White Skull Snow Mountain," a famous peak near Lhasa.

17 A vast collection of Dzogchen Upadesha teachings, some of which were composed by Longchenpa, while others were compiled by him.

But our present condition is not like this. If we do a retreat in a city, many people come, and some may be genuinely interested, but others are not. It is not so easy for the teacher to check everybody one by one, but whether or not all students are serious, the teacher should give teachings in a serious way. Then he is connected to all students by *samaya*, and later, if they are ignorant and do not treat one another with respect but argue and create problems, this is not good at all, and is also bad for the teacher. But if you are a teacher in that position, what can you do?

Sometimes I feel very sad because I cannot leave my students or refuse to teach them when they ask for teachings. So then we go ahead, and of course we have so many of these kinds of problems. Then I do not know what to do. So this is why Longchenpa is saying we should do our best to remain alone and do practice.

Practicing in Solitude

།སྔོན་གྱི་སྐྱེ་བོ་དམ་པ་མཆོག་རྣམས་ཀྱང་།
།དབེན་པར་གནས་ལས་བདུད་རྩི་བརྙེས་ཞེས་གསུངས།
།དེ་ཕྱིར་བདག་ཀྱང་ཞི་བ་སྒྲུབ་པའི་ཕྱིར།
།ནགས་ནང་དབེན་པ་གཅིག་པུར་གནས་པར་བྱ།

The supreme holy beings of the past have said
They found the nectar [of realization] by abiding
in solitude.
So I too will remain alone in the solitude of the forest
In order to accomplish the state of peace.

In ancient times many practitioners and realized beings spent their lives like this, doing personal retreat and living in quiet places, and finally attaining realization. So for this reason, Longchenpa says he is going to follow their example and remain alone in retreat, and spend his entire life in the state of contemplation.

How should we apply this kind of advice? Many people hear about practitioners like Milarepa and then they want to go alone into the mountains and be like him. But in our human condition only very few people really have that opportunity. Even if we have the intention, it does not usually correspond with our circumstances. For example, if we have children, we cannot abandon them. In this case, what should we do?

If we are Dzogchen practitioners, we do not necessarily need to be alone for many years to have realization. To follow the Vajrayana path, for example, we need to stay in retreat for a long time, because we cannot really apply those practice methods in only a few weeks or months. That is why many practitioners in Tibet do retreat for seven years. When you dedicate seven years in retreat to these Vajrayana practices, maybe you can succeed. Also we have many places for three-year retreats for the same reason.

But if we are following the Dzogchen teachings, our main practice is being in the state of contemplation, also called instant presence. This means being in our real nature, which we are directly introduced to by our teacher. To develop our capacity to be in this state, it is not necessary for us to remain in retreat for many years.

In the state of contemplation, there is nothing to concentrate on, nothing to meditate on with our mind. Vajrayana uses meditation on a deity as a method to find a state of contemplation. But in the real sense, our nature is beyond any color or form. In the Dzogchen teachings, we use the symbol of Samantabhadra to represent our real nature. Samantabhadra is presented as totally naked and without any ornaments because our real nature is beyond all form.

At the same time, he appears like a human being with one head, two arms, and two legs. However, this is only to show his relation to ourselves: right now we are human beings, so a human body is a symbol that is familiar in our dimension. In the real sense, Samantabhadra is beyond form, but he is presented in the form of a human being to show that his state is our own state. If we were elephants, for example, he would be presented in the form of an elephant.

Samantabhadra is shown sitting in a position of meditation, which represents that we can discover our real condition when we are in the meditation state. He is blue in color to represent the state of very deep emptiness. Although space has no color, when we look into the sky on a very clear day, it manifests as the color blue. So in the same way, to represent the state of emptiness beyond any color, Samantabhadra is shown as being blue.

In any case, when you discover your real nature and can remain in this state even for a few minutes or seconds, this is called the state of contemplation. Once you have real knowledge of it, to develop your capacity to integrate with this state you can do a one- or two-month retreat, or even a retreat of just a few weeks, and it can serve as a kind of preparation for integrating the state of contemplation into your daily life.

It is just like learning how to swim. We cannot just jump into the water with all our clothes on. First we should prepare well, and then we can swim without a problem. This is how we should understand the principle of retreat according to the Dzogchen teachings. In order to practice Dzogchen, we do not need to change our situation; we do not need to renounce anything. If we develop our capacity to integrate, we can have a normal life and still be perfect Dzogchen practitioners. This is why it is said that the Dzogchen teachings will remain in our dimension after all other teachings have disappeared. Some Dzogchen Upadesha tantras explain that even when human beings have very short lives and this Earth is near the point of total destruction, the Dzogchen teachings will still exist. Why? Because Dzogchen is not much related to outer conditions. Whatever our outer situation is, as Dzogchen practitioners we can always integrate our practice into that situation.

Of course, if you want to be alone in retreat for a long time and you have the opportunity to do so, this is also fine. Not only Sutrayana or Vajrayana practitioners, but also many Dzogchen practitioners go off alone and stay in retreat for their whole lives. But it is much more important for us to be aware of our situation and not pursue fantasies.

If you leave your family and quit your job, sell your house and your possessions, and with that money go to do a three-year retreat, maybe you think everything will be okay because anyway, after three years, you will have realization. But three years pass quickly, and after three years you are more or less the same as you were before. The only difference is that now you have no house, no family, and no job. Then what can you do? Maybe you decide to do another three-year retreat, but afterward, if you are still alive, you will have the same problem again. So it is much better to work with our real situation and not follow after our fantasies.

།དབེན་པའི་གནས་ནི་རྒྱལ་བ་རྣམས་ཀྱིས་བསྔགས།
།མི་སྲུན་མི་མེད་ཟབ་མོའི་ཏིང་འཛིན་འཕེལ།
།ངང་གིས་ཆོས་འགྲུབ་མི་རྟག་སྐྱོ་ཤེས་སྐྱེ།
།ཡོ་བྱད་སྤྱངས་ཤིང་འདུ་འཛི་རྣམ་གཡེང་མེད།
།དད་དང་ངེས་འབྱུང་ཡོན་ཏན་ཚོགས་མང་ཞིང་།
།འབྲེལ་འདྲིས་མེད་པས་ངང་གིས་བྱ་བ་ཞུང་།

Places of solitude are praised by the conquerors:
Far from rough people,
    profound contemplation flourishes,

The Dharma is accomplished naturally, and disillusionment
arises toward impermanent phenomena.
You cast off your possessions and remain
without the diversion of worldly endeavors.
You amass abundant good qualities of faith
and renunciation,
And without ties to others your tasks naturally become few.

Here we have some more detailed explanations about the advantages of being alone in retreat. When we remain in a peaceful, quiet place where there is no one to create problems for us, many good qualities can arise and automatically increase. For example, our awareness of impermanence, our feelings of devotion, and our sense of sadness about samsara can all arise naturally and spontaneously. And if we are beginners and have not yet stabilized our ability to integrate with movement, being in retreat also allows us to enter more deeply into the state of contemplation and develop that capacity.

Then our faith in the teachings also increases, and we naturally have less and less interest in ordinary activities. So apart from practice we have very few things to do, and as time goes on, our activities become more and more integrated with our practice of Dharma. When we can be like this, it means we are seriously doing retreat and our practice is having a good effect.

།གཞན་གྱི་སེམས་འཛིན་ངོ་སྲུང་ཆོས་བརྒྱད་མེད།
།རང་དབང་འགྱུར་བདེ་ཉེན་མཚན་ཆོས་ཀྱིས་འདའ།
།དལ་འབྱོར་དོན་ཡོད་སྒྲུབ་པ་སྙིང་པོར་བྱེད།
།དེ་སོགས་ཡོན་ཏན་བརྗོད་ཀྱིས་མི་ལང་བས།
།གཅིག་པུར་རབ་ཏུ་དབེན་པའི་ནགས་ཁྲོད་དུ།
།ཚེ་གང་ཟབ་མོའི་ཏིང་འཛིན་བསྒྲུབ་པར་བྱ།

With no need to please others or to save face,
    and free from the eight worldly concerns,
You have the fortune and joy of independence,
    and pass day and night in the practice of Dharma.
You give meaning to your condition of freedom
    and advantage by applying the essence of the practice.
These and other qualities of solitude exceed description,
So remain alone in the perfect solitude of the forest
Practicing profound contemplation for the rest
    of your life.

When we are alone in retreat, we do not need to think about how other people want us to behave or not behave, so of course we can generally be more free. Day and night, we can integrate everything – our body, speech, and mind – with our practice, which means we are seriously using our precious human condition for having realization, and making this our main priority.

།དེ་ལྟར་ལེགས་གསུང་ཆོས་ཀྱི་ཆར་བསིལ་བས།
།ཉོན་མོངས་གདུང་བའི་རྟོག་པ་རབ་ཞི་ནས།
།ཏིང་འཛིན་དགེ་ཚོགས་པད་མཚོ་རབ་གང་སྟེ།
།ཞི་བའི་གནས་ན་འབྱོར་པ་རབ་རྒྱས་ཤོག

May this cooling rain of well-spoken Dharma
Completely pacify the thoughts that burn you in the heat
    of emotions;
May it fill the lotus lake of the gathering of contemplation
    and virtue,
And in this place of peace, may fortune reach full blossom.

།ཆོས་བཞི་རིན་པོ་ཆེའི་ཕྲེང་བ་ལས།
།བློ་ཆོས་སུ་འགྲོ་བའི་རབས་ཏེ་དང་པོའོ།

From *The Precious Mala of the Four Dharmas,* this is the first teaching, on turning your mind to the Dharma.

Samsaric beings are always suffering from the heat of emotions, and this teaching is something like a gentle rain to help us feel relief from that heat. Then, as this rain falls, our state of contemplation and our accumulations of merit bloom like many lotus flowers in a lake, and everything auspicious manifests in this dimension of perfect peace.

This is Longchenpa's explanation of how we can turn our minds to the Dharma. In the Dzogchen teachings, when we speak of whether or not a person has the capacity to follow the teachings, we say that the most important qualification is to have genuine interest, because without this we will never actively apply the teachings in our daily lives, which means we will never actually step onto the path.

Many people live in a passive way because it is easier. They might think, "There is no need to sacrifice my time and energy to do practice. I can go to a great teacher, and he can give me enlightenment!" Some people even think they can buy enlightenment with offerings of money.

Everything would be much easier if this were possible, but it is not. Buddha never said, "Your realization depends on me, so have faith in me and I will give you realization." What he said was, "I can show you the path, but your realization depends on you." This is why it is really important for us to cultivate our interest, so that we can become more active in applying the teachings. Cultivating this capacity of interest is the real meaning of directing our mind to the Dharma.

The Second Dharma:

Taking the Dharma as a Path

།དེ་ལྟར་རབ་དཀར་དམ་པའི་ཆོས་མཆོག་ལ།
།དད་པས་རབ་ཞུགས་ཐར་ལམ་འདོད་རྣམས་ཀྱིས།
།རང་གི་སེམས་ཉིད་རབ་ཏུ་གདུལ་བྱའི་ཕྱིར།
།ཆོས་དེ་ལམ་དུ་འགྲོ་བ་རབ་ཏུ་གཅེས།

Having entered, through faith, into this pure, sacred,
and supreme Dharma,
It is most crucial for those of you who long [to travel]
the path to liberation,
To take this Dharma as a path
In order to thoroughly tame your minds.

ONCE WE HAVE the interest and wish to apply the teachings, we need to know how to actually do this so that our practice of Dharma becomes a path to realization. A path is something we walk on to get somewhere. So taking the Dharma as our path means making it something concrete in our life, something that actually functions for us.

In Dzogchen we say that if we want to make use of what we have learned, we must integrate this knowledge into our daily life. If we are always distracted and do not succeed in integrating the teachings, it is like seeing a path in front of us but not traveling on it.

In general, our minds are always distracted, and this creates many problems for us. So if you have faith in the Dharma and seriously want to apply it, the first thing you must do is govern your mind with awareness so that you do not remain distracted. This will enable your knowledge of Dharma to become something concrete.

Avoiding Faults and Deviations

།འདི་ལྟར་རྒྱལ་བའི་བསྟན་ལ་རབ་ཞུགས་ནས།
།ཐོས་བསམ་སྒོམ་པར་ཆས་པ་དེ་དག་ཀྱང་།
།ཁ་ཅིག་མ་ཞི་རང་རྒྱུད་ངན་པ་དང་།
།ལ་ལ་ལམ་ལོག་དམན་དང་ལམ་གོལ་ཞུགས།

Even among those who have entered the teachings
of the conquerors
And have begun to listen, reflect, and meditate upon them,
Some remain restless, in negative states of mind,
While others stray onto perverse, inferior, or mistaken paths.

When we follow the teachings of Buddha and want to achieve the fruit of total realization, we begin by studying, then we analyze and think about what we have studied and try to become familiar with all the different methods of applying the teachings. Then, finally, we apply these methods and enter into the state of meditation. This is the general order in which we should approach the teachings.

However, even after beginning in this way and going through these stages, many people do not succeed in integrating the real sense of the teachings in their condition. They do not find a calm state, but instead develop an even more negative character than before, and behave in ways that are totally contrary to the Dharma. Or sometimes, they apply incorrect methods that do not bring them closer to realization, but still they think, "I am a great scholar, I have studied very deeply, and my opinions definitely correspond to the way things are." Such people may even invent something entirely new and teach it to others.

།འདོད་སྲེད་ཆེ་དང་ཚེ་འདིར་གཡེངས་ལ་སོགས།
།ཆོས་དང་འགལ་བའི་ཉེས་པ་དེ་དག་ཀུན།
།ཆོས་དེ་ལམ་དུ་མ་སོང་དག་ལས་བྱུང་།

Being strongly conditioned by cravings and desires,
        preoccupied with the concerns of this life,
And all other such faults that contradict the Dharma
Arise from your not having applied this Dharma as a path.

If our way of understanding or applying the Dharma is not correct, we can develop strong attachments and desires for worldly things. For example, we can feel the desire to become famous or to gain a position higher than that of others. Then, in order to satisfy this desire, we do many things that are contrary to the real sense of the Dharma.

།དེ་ལས་འདི་ཕྱིའི་ཉེས་པ་ཚད་མེད་དེ།
།འཁྲུལ་པས་བསླུས་གང་འཆི་ཁར་འགྱོད་པ་ཉིད།
།བར་དོར་འཇིགས་དངངས་ཕྱི་མར་ངན་སོང་འགྲོ།
།གཏན་དུ་སྲིད་ལས་ཐར་པའི་སྐབས་མེད་དོ།
།དེ་བས་ཆོས་དེ་ལམ་དུ་འགྲོ་བར་བྱ།

This leads to problems beyond measure,
        both in this life and the next.
Those who are deceived by illusions
        have only regret at the moment of death,

Terror and panic in the intermediate state,
and rebirth in the realms of misery:
They never have the chance to free themselves
from samsara.
This is why you must apply the Dharma as a path.

If we keep going in this direction and let ourselves be dominated by illusion, we will experience many negative things in this life, and our situation will also be very negative in future lives.

When we are conditioned by illusion, we might remain in this state day after day without even caring or thinking about it. Then one day we arrive at the end of our life and suddenly realize that we did not do particularly well. But by then it is too late to do anything about it. So we enter the *bardo* state full of fear, and after the *bardo* we find ourselves in one of the three lower realms, where we can continue to circle endlessly and never liberate ourselves from samsara.

།ཇི་ལྟར་ནད་ཀྱི་གཉེན་པོར་མི་དག་གིས།
།བཀྲུ་སྨན་སྐྱུར་ཡང་དེ་ཉིད་མ་དག་ན།
།ཡོངས་སུ་གདུང་བས་སྡར་ལ་གདུངས་པ་བཞིན།
།གཉེན་པོར་མ་སོང་ཆོས་ལ་དགོས་པ་ཅི།
།འདི་ན་དེ་འདྲའི་ཉེས་པ་ཚད་མེད་པས།
།དད་ལྡན་སྐྱེ་བོས་ལེགས་པར་ཤེས་པར་བྱ།

If the remedy for an illness is used incorrectly,
Though applied as a salve it is toxic instead,
Causing great pain that only prolongs your torment.
Likewise, what use is the Dharma if it does not serve as a
remedy?
If misapplied, it will cause immeasurable harm,

So those with faith must understand this well.

It is crucially important that whatever Dharma we learn becomes something concrete for us, that it actually becomes our path. This means that from the time we first begin to receive teachings, we must try to not just remain on the level of intellectual knowledge but to understand their real sense.

For example, when we discover that we have an illness, we usually use some kind of medicine so we can get better. A medicine is an antidote to an illness. But if we use a medicine incorrectly and it creates problems for us instead of curing our illness, it can no longer be called medicine. Instead, it has become a poison.

In the same way, we may have learned some Dharma, but if we do not integrate it in our own condition so that it manifests as a concrete experience, not only will it be of no benefit, it can actually create infinite problems for us. So if we are really going to dedicate ourselves to this path, we must understand these things, and always do our best to be aware and apply the real sense of the teachings in our life.

Following a Qualified Teacher

།དེ་ལ་ཆོས་དེ་ལམ་དུ་འགྲོ་བ་ནི།
།ཐོག་མར་དགེ་བའི་བཤེས་ལ་རག་ལས་པས།
།མཚན་ལྡན་བླ་མ་དམ་པ་བསྟེན་པ་གཅེས།
།དེ་ལས་ལེགས་རྒྱུའི་ཡོན་ཏན་དུ་མ་འབྱུང་།

Applying the Dharma as a path depends, before all else,
On having a teacher of virtue.
So it is crucial to rely upon a sublime qualified master,
The source of myriad excellent qualities.

From the beginning, knowing how to apply the teachings in the right way depends very much on whether you are following a qualified teacher, one who has real knowledge and applies that knowledge in a way that perfectly corresponds to the path. This kind of teacher can be truly beneficial and can help you manifest many good qualities.

On the other hand, we must also be aware that not all who call themselves teachers are like this. Many people jump into a relationship with a teacher before examining him, just because he has an important name, a powerful position in a monastery, or a nice way of speaking. This is a mistake. We must remember that we are now living in the Kaliyuga,[18] and in the Kaliyuga we commonly find people who are not what they claim to be. It is a period of time when anything can happen. So you must not assume that someone is an enlightened being just because he has the title of *rinpoche* or *trulku.*

We say that Buddha Shakyamuni is a *nirmanakaya* buddha, or *trulku*[19] in Tibetan. This means he appears as a teacher in a human body so we can have direct contact with him and can listen to his teachings. But although he manifests in a human form, he is actually a fully realized being who has taken birth in our dimension freely, rather than as a result of karma.

Ordinary people take rebirth by the power of their karma. As we know, Buddha said, "To see what you have done in your past life, observe your present body. To see what kind of rebirth you will take in the

---

18 According to Buddhist cosmology, a *kaliyuga* is the final dark age of an aeon (Skt. *kalpa*) preceding the destruction of the physical universe and its dissolution into a state of pure potential, out of which the physical universe reemerges at the start of the next aeon. See Jamgön Kongtrul Lodrö Thaye, *Myriad Worlds.*
19 Literally "emanated body."

future, observe your present actions." So this means the circumstances of our rebirth are related very closely to our karma.

When we refer to somebody as a *trulku,* it means we consider that they are no longer subject to karma in this way. At least this is what we think. But particularly in Tibet, most so-called *trulkus* are given this title only to benefit a monastery. When I was in monastic college, I was the only student with this title, and my teacher would always warn me, "A monastery that has a *trulku* is like a family that acquires a rich wife." Traditionally, in India, a family is not happy when a girl is born, because when she grows up and gets married, she must go to live with her husband's family and her parents must give that family a large sum of money as a gift, or else they will not accept her. On the other hand, if a boy is born, his family is very happy because later this boy will have a wife, and a wife means money for the family. Of course, if they can, they will find him a wife from a rich family, because a wife from a rich family brings more money than one from a poor family. In the same way, if you do a little research into Tibetan history, you will see that when monasteries search for their lamas' reincarnations, they usually find them in rich or important families.

On the other hand, if he is not rich, even an authentic reincarnation may experience many difficulties. This is true even for very important or high level reincarnations. For example, when the Fifteenth Karmapa passed away, his reincarnation was found in Derge, eastern Tibet. He was recognized as the Sixteenth Karmapa by Tai Situpa and most other important lamas of the Karma Kagyüd school, and they performed his coronation ceremony at Palpung Monastery. But Derge is far from the Karmapa's main residence of Tsurpu, which is in central Tibet near Lhasa, and at that time in central Tibet some lamas identified another boy as the Karmapa, a boy from an extremely powerful family connected to the central government in Lhasa.

As soon as he was recognized, this family brought this boy to Tsurpu, where they held his coronation ceremony. So the Sixteenth Karmapa could not go to his main residence, and had to stay at Palpung Monastery. Even when this other boy fell from the roof of Tsurpu and died at the age of seventeen, the Karmapa was not allowed to go to his residence, because the boy's family and the central government in Lhasa would not give him permission.

Finally, when the Karmapa was about twenty-three years old, many Kagyüd monasteries in Derge, as well as the king of Derge, sent large sums of money and expensive gifts to the central government, which then gave permission and officially recognized the Karmapa, who was finally allowed to go to Tsurpu. There are many stories like this.

Sometimes a *trulku* will manifest many signs and qualifications at a very young age, and then we can say he is a real *trulku*. For example, some *trulkus* have a very profound knowledge of the teachings even without having to study like ordinary people. On the other hand, some boys are recognized as *trulkus* and assigned multiple teachers who beat them every day because they do not study or understand well, but they still remain stupid.

So we must not follow a teacher only because he is called a *trulku*. Not only are there good and bad teachers with this title, there are also some people who are not recognized and have no title at all but manifest extraordinary qualities. This is why we should always use our intelligence, open our eyes, and try to see for ourselves whether or not someone is manifesting the qualities of a teacher in a concrete way.

།དེ་ཡང་ཐབས་མཁས་ཐུགས་རྗེའི་བདག་ཉིད་ཅན།

Such a master is adept in skillful methods,
and is the very embodiment of compassion.

A teacher must know how to apply any methods that might be useful to his students according to their circumstances. It is not enough to guide people according to a set of instructions or rules, because something fixed like this is limited and will not always correspond to a student's personal situation or to the conditions in his country or culture.

For example, before Guru Padmasambhava came to Tibet, King Trisong Deutsen[20] had already invited Shantarakshita to come and teach Buddhism to the Tibetans. Shantarakshita was a great scholar, and in particular, he had a profound knowledge of Sutrayana, so when he arrived in Tibet this is what he began to teach. But the Tibetans were not interested in these Sutra teachings, and eventually they even turned against Shantarakshita. This was because at that time the Tibetans already had the Bön religion, and Shantarakshita's teaching had no connection to Bön. Modern Bön has everything that Buddhism has, but this was not the case with ancient Bön.[21] Practitioners of ancient Bön mainly practiced rituals dealing with nature and the elements, and they had a deep knowledge of these things. But there were no Sutrayana teachings, no Bönpo monks, and no teachings on celibacy or monasticism, so the teachings of Shantarakshita did not correspond at all with their knowledge or culture.

Eventually, Shantarakshita became upset and decided to go to Nepal. But before he left, he told the king that if he wanted to establish Buddhism in Tibet he should invite Padmasambhava. Since Guru Padmasambhava was mainly a teacher of Vajrayana, he was able to give teachings related to the principle of energy and the elements.

---

20 Second of the three great Dharma kings of Tibet.

21 See Chögyal Namkhai Norbu, *Drung, Deu, and Bon.*

Guru Padmasambhava was also a great teacher of Dzogchen, and in Dzogchen the fundamental principle is not to change anything but to integrate with everything as it is. For this reason, he had a profound understanding of how to communicate with people in diverse situations. So when he began to teach the Tibetans, he used the outer form of many aspects of the Bön tradition that people were already familiar with to communicate knowledge of the principles of Vajrayana Buddhism. By teaching in this way, he attracted people's interest and many of his students became great practitioners. This is an example of what it means to be adept at using skillful methods.

Another important qualification is that a teacher must base his actions on authentic compassion rather than on self-interest. This means he should be ready to make real sacrifices for his students.

།ཞི་ཞིང་དུལ་བ་བཟོད་དང་ལྡན་པ་སྟེ།

He is calm, disciplined, and patient.

A teacher should have a calm and peaceful nature, which means he does not have many tensions or problems in his life. He should be capable of being truly patient with his students. If he needs to explain something ten or twenty times before a student manifests real knowledge and understanding, a good teacher will never refuse or think, "This is a bad student; he is not worth my time."

།སྡོམ་དང་དམ་ཚིག་སྤྱོད་ཚུལ་ཕུན་སུམ་ཚོགས།

His way of applying the vows and *samayas* is perfect and complete.

A teacher's behavior should perfectly correspond to the essence of his vows and *samayas*.

།མང་དུ་ཐོས་ཤིང་ལེགས་པར་སྦྱངས་པ་ཆེ།

His learning is vast, his training excellent and thorough.

It is not sufficient to know only one aspect or part of the teachings, or to understand one book, and then imagine that you have the capacity to be a teacher. A teacher must have knowledge of the different levels of teachings, different schools, and so on. Even someone who is mainly teaching Dzogchen must know everything about Sutrayana and Vajrayana as well.

།བྱིན་རླབས་ཚད་མེད་གཞན་སྣང་རང་གིས་འགྱུར།

His immeasurable blessings naturally transform the vision
of others.

A qualified teacher has real blessings that the student can receive through his teachings. Having blessings means he has real knowledge and has integrated this knowledge in his condition. Also, he has the ability to transform others from ordinary people into people who have knowledge just like him.

།ཚེ་འདི་མ་འདྲེས་ཆོས་བརྒྱད་མཁའ་ལྟར་དག

He is not entangled in the affairs of this life,
and is as pure of the eight worldly dharmas as space itself.

To be conditioned by the eight worldly dharmas[22] means that everything you do is motivated by ego and self-interest. A good teacher has no interest in these things and is not conditioned by them.

།འབྲེལ་ཚད་དོན་ལྡན་ཐར་ལམ་འགོད་པ་འདི།
།སྙིགས་མའི་དུས་སུ་རྒྱལ་བའི་རྣམ་འཕྲུལ་ཏེ།
།རབ་དང་གུས་པ་ཆེན་པོས་བསྟེན་པར་བྱ།

Any connection made with him is meaningful
and establishes you on the path to liberation.
Such a master is a manifestation of the Conqueror in these degenerate times,
So rely on him with a pure mind and the highest respect.

Any connection with an enlightened being, or even with somebody who is seriously on the path, is a cause for us to have total realization whether our present relationship with him is good or bad. Of course, a good relationship is much better than a bad one. But any karmic connection with someone like this means we have the opportunity to receive wisdom from him, whether now or at some future time. Receiving wisdom means we have the opportunity to enter the path, and being on the path means we will eventually have total realization. In this sense, even a bad relationship with an authentic teacher is never truly bad.

This is why Longchenpa says that such a teacher is like an emanation of the Buddha in this degenerate time of the Kaliyuga. So if we examine him and find that our teacher really does have these qualities,

22 The eight worldly dharmas are to pursue personal gain, fame, praise, and pleasure, and to avoid loss, disrepute, blame, and pain.

we should pay him great respect and follow him with confidence and devotion.

།དེ་ལས་ཕན་ཡོན་ཚད་མེད་ཟད་མེད་དེ།
།སྲིད་ལ་སྐྱོ་ཞིང་ངེས་འབྱུང་བློ་སྣ་ཐུང་།
།ཚེ་འདི་བློས་ཐོངས་འཁྲུལ་སྣང་བདག་འཛིན་འཇིག
།ངང་གིས་དུལ་ཞིང་ཐོས་བསམ་སྒོམ་པ་ལྡན།
།དད་སོགས་རྒྱ་ཆེ་སྦྱངས་པའི་ཡོན་ཏན་ལྡན།
།ཚེ་འདི་དོན་ཡོད་ཕྱི་མ་འབྲས་དང་བཅས།
།དེ་ཕྱིར་དམ་པ་རྣམས་ལ་བསྟེན་པར་བྱ།

The benefits of doing so are immeasurable
and inexhaustible:
Disillusioned with samsara, you renounce it and curtail
your plans;
You cast away thoughts of this present life, and your
clinging to the reality of illusory vision collapses;
You become naturally disciplined, and are endowed
with listening, reflection, and meditation.
Possessing faith and myriad other qualities of training,
Your present life becomes truly meaningful, and in future
lives you will experience the fruits of this.
This is why you should rely on sublime masters.

Many benefits arise from following this kind of teacher. For example, we begin to feel a genuine sadness about transmigration, because we understand that samsara is infinitely full of sentient beings experiencing infinite kinds of suffering, and most of them have no guarantee of one day being free from this situation.

Understanding this makes us lose interest in worldly things, so we engage in fewer activities that serve only ourselves and only in this present life. Instead, we apply ourselves to activities that will benefit us in future lives and benefit all sentient beings.

Once we have the presence of knowing that everything is impermanent, we are able to start letting go of our illusory karmic vision and our ego; even if we have a very strong ego, we are at least aware of this and try to go beyond this condition.

When we have such knowledge of the real sense of the teachings, these benefits manifest in us naturally, without our having to use any effort to think about or cultivate them; they also arise in us when we study the teachings, reflect on them, and apply them in meditation. In this way, all qualities manifest in us and we obtain many benefits even in this life, but particularly in future lives.

།དེ་ཡང་རང་གི་སྒོ་གསུམ་ཟོལ་མེད་པས།
།ནད་པས་སྨན་པ་ཚོང་པས་དེད་དཔོན་དང་།
།གྲུ་པས་མཉན་པ་མགྲོན་པོས་སྐྱེལ་མ་ལྟར།
།གུས་པའི་སྲི་ཞུས་རྟག་ཏུ་མཉེས་པར་བྱ།

In this regard, without deception or artifice in your three
gates,
Be like a patient with his doctor, a merchant with his captain,
A passenger with his ferryman, and a traveler with his guide,
And always please your master with respectful
and devoted service.

It is not enough to have a qualified teacher; we must also follow him correctly. We must be respectful and devote ourselves to our teacher in a genuine way with body, speech, and mind, and not just pretend or make a show of doing so. Here we have some examples of what this looks like.

The first example is that of a patient with his doctor. When we have confidence in a doctor, first we go to him and request information in order to understand the nature of our illness. Our doctor prescribes the medicine we need to take and also explains how we can live in a healthier way. Then, when we have received all this information and apply it in a concrete way, we overcome our illness.

The next example is that of a trader on a ship with his leader or captain. In ancient times, people sometimes travelled extremely long distances to do business. We can read in the sutras about people who sailed across the ocean to reach islands containing jewels and precious stones. On this kind of journey, a large group of people would rely on one person who knew the way, and they depended on him completely, because without this leader they could not arrive at their destination or return safely home.

This example represents our situation very closely, and for this reason we often say in the Dzogchen teachings that all of us who are connected through the Dzogchen transmission are together in the same boat. Why do we use the example of a boat? Because we are in samsara, and samsara is like a vast ocean that we are trying to cross. On a boat, if even one person creates a problem, it becomes a problem for everybody else as well. So if the people travelling together on a boat wish to reach their destination, they must always collaborate and work well together and, in particular, they need to precisely follow the captain's instructions.

Even if we are only trying to reach the other side of a river, it is not so easy if we cannot swim. And even if we can swim, it is often impossible to safely swim across. In such a case, we need to cross in a small boat or ferry with the help of a capable sailor or ferryman. We should rely on our teacher in the same way a ferry passenger relies on his ferryman.

The final example is that if we are travelling in a foreign country and do not know how to get around, we should rely on a guide who is fully familiar with that place. If you have great confidence in your own intellectual capacity and logic, you might decide to just use a map rather than rely on an experienced guide, but if you do this, the outcome is never certain.

For example, once I was travelling in Nepal with a group of Westerners. We were in the mountains, and had hired some Nepali and Sherpa porters to carry our bags, some of which were very heavy. These porters knew the way very well, so they were also showing us which path to take. But at one point some people in our group were looking at their map and saying, "Look, there's a more direct road than the one we are taking. We should go that way instead." The porters told us that the road there was not good at all, but some of these people insisted on taking that route, so they took some porters with them and separated from our group.

The rest of us decided to follow the porters' advice. We reached our destination that same day, and waited there for the other group to arrive. But it took that group four days to get there, because the path they had taken was very difficult and steep, and after two days the porters they had taken with them refused to go further and left them there to carry their own things. This is an example of what can happen when we rely on our own logic instead of the knowledge of those with direct experience.

So if we are seriously trying to enter the path and apply the teachings, we should not behave like this. Instead, we should be humble and pay respect to our teacher, knowing that his advice is more valuable than our own logic and intellectual understanding.

།མ་དད་ལོག་པར་ལྟ་བའི་སེམས་སྐྱེས་ན།
།སྐད་ཅིག་གྲངས་བཞིན་ངན་འགྲོར་འཇུག་པར་གསུངས།
།དེ་བས་བཤགས་སྡོམ་འགྱོད་ཚངས་ཆེན་པོ་ཡིས།
།དམ་ཚིག་རྣམ་དག་མིག་བཞིན་བསྲུང་ལ་འབད།

It is said that you will enter the lower realms
As many times as the number of moments for which you
hold a faithless, perverse view of your teacher.
So guard the purity of your *samayas* as you would your
own eyes
By confessing [faults] with great remorse
and vowing [to not repeat them].

Some people start out with a perfect relationship with their teacher, but later on they lose confidence and start thinking their teacher is no good. This situation produces very heavy karma, and Buddha taught that it is a cause for students to take rebirth in the lower realms. To avoid this, it is extremely important to keep your eyes open and examine a teacher before deciding to follow him. If, after investigating, you see that he is a qualified teacher after all, you can follow him and will not have this problem.

When a teacher comes to a Western country to give teachings or empowerments, people often attend without knowing anything about him. Maybe it is because there are not many teachers coming to their country, and they think, "I need to receive this teaching." But after they receive empowerment and get to know him, they might lose sight of his qualities even if he is a good teacher, and then decide that they do not like him after all. Or he might in fact be a bad teacher for some reason.

For example, one thing we can see manifesting in the Kaliyuga is many people doing Dharma business, presenting themselves as teachers even if they have no qualifications. When people want to make money this way, it is not at all difficult for them to present themselves as teachers and deceive others. Many people are happy when they see a teacher with a nice appearance and beautiful robes, and without knowing anything apart from how he dresses, they take him for a serious teacher. This is why teachers who have no qualifications often present themselves in a beautiful and elegant way, and gather many students around them.

When these students discover that their teacher not good, they might become angry and decide to publicly criticize their teacher or to write an article or book explaining his faults. This is very bad. If you enter blindly into a relationship with a teacher before examining his qualifications, and later discover that he is not qualified, this is your own fault, not the fault of the teacher. It does not give you a reason to criticize or be angry at him.

If you have already created a relationship and then discover that your teacher is not good, you can separate from him because you no longer need him, but do not hold onto negative thoughts about him, and do not criticize him. If you do, and if you act in a way that goes against what he taught you, this is very negative, and poses a serious obstacle to realization, regardless of whether your teacher is in fact good or bad.

In particular, behaving like this toward a teacher from whom you have received Vajrayana transmission breaks your *samaya*, because having *samaya* means always maintaining the idea that this teacher is an enlightened being. As Guru Padmasambhava said, if you see your teacher as a totally realized being, you will achieve the state of a totally realized being; if you see him as an ordinary person, you can only attain that state, and if you see him as a dog, you attain that state. He did not say this in order to support his position as a teacher, but because it is actually true and he wanted his students to achieve realization. This is also why Longchenpa says that we should protect our *samaya* as carefully as we protect our own eyes, and if we break it, we must purify that negativity and do our best to keep *samaya* from then on.

The best way to keep pure *samaya* with all your teachers is to practice Guruyoga. There are different systems employing visualizations, invocations, and so on, but in the Dzogchen teachings, once you receive transmission from a qualified teacher, the way to practice the essence of Guruyoga is to be in your real nature, in the state of instant presence, which is the unification state of all your teachers.

If you want to practice Guruyoga in a more Vajrayana style, you can also visualize the unification state of all your teachers in front of you in the form of Guru Padmasambhava, Guru Garab Dorje, Samantabhadra, Vajrasattva, or any other enlightened being, and then unify with that state. But whatever form you visualize, the most important thing is to consider that that figure represents the unification of all your teachers and all enlightened beings.

This is how Guru Padmasambhava taught the practice of Guruyoga. You should not be worried about whether it is appropriate to unify all your teachers in the state of Guruyoga, even if they come from different traditions, and even if some of them have themselves said that mixing different traditions is negative and will lead to confusion. Some people think, "If I unify my Gelugpa teachers, Nyingmapa teachers, and Bönpo teachers, maybe they will not like being together and it will be negative." People often have such ideas. But in the practice of Guruyoga, you must consider all your teachers to be totally enlightened beings, otherwise there is no reason to do this practice. If your teachers are totally enlightened beings, this means they are beyond all such limitations and problems. For this reason, we should also try to get beyond these limitations ourselves.

There is another important reason to practice Guruyoga in this way. Many of us have taken many Vajrayana initiations, and whenever we take an initiation we receive a practice commitment connected to a particular *yidam,* or wisdom deity. Today, when teachers give initiations, many of them say not to worry about this, that it is only a kind of blessing without any commitment. But this is not true. If you only want a blessing, why not just ask your teacher to give you a blessing in a normal way, by putting a statue or a book on your head and saying some mantras? If you feel like you need a more powerful blessing, you can ask him to put the book on your head ten or twenty times. But in an initiation, the teacher enters into the transformation state of a particular deity, then introduces the student to this state and empowers the student's transformation with the potentiality of mantra. This means you are now connected to this teacher and this deity through the Vajrayana transmission, and this always involves a commitment.

If you have taken twenty initiations, you have twenty different commitments, and not keeping these commitments becomes an obstacle to your realization. According to the general Vajrayana tradition, the way to keep these commitments is to do all the practices you have received on a daily basis. Of course, if you have received many initiations and try to fulfill your commitments in this way, you will not have time to do anything else.

But we can apply a different approach according to the principle of the Dzogchen teachings. In Dzogchen we say that our teacher, and not the deity, is most important, because it is from our teacher and not from the deity that we receive an initiation. For this reason, when we practice Guruyoga and unify ourselves with the state of all our teachers, this is the essence of all *samaya* commitments. This is the Dzogchen way, not the way of Vajrayana in general.

Integrating the Dharma in Daily Life

།དེ་ལྟར་བཤེས་གཉེན་དམ་པ་རབ་བསྟེན་ནས།
།ཐོས་བསམ་སྒོམ་པས་རང་རྒྱུད་སྦྱངས་བྱས་ནས།
།ཐར་པ་ཁོ་ན་འདོད་པའི་བསམ་པ་ཡིས།
།གང་བྱེད་དགེ་བ་འདུན་པས་བསྒྱུར་བ་ནི།
།ཆོས་དེ་ལམ་དུ་འགྲོ་བའི་མན་ངག་ཡིན།

Having come to rely in this way upon a sublime teacher
of virtue,
And having trained your mind through listening, reflection,
and meditation,
Transform everything you do into the pursuit
of virtue
By thinking only of the desire for liberation.
This is the quintessential instruction
for applying the Dharma as a path.

If we have a perfect teacher, we can receive perfect teachings, enter a perfect path, and have perfect realization. So the first step for us is to find a perfect teacher. Then we listen to his teachings, think about them, and try to understand their meaning. Finally, we apply these teachings in meditation, which means we integrate what we have learned so that our own condition corresponds to the real sense of the Dharma. Then everything we do will be in accord with the teachings, because all of our actions are motivated only by our desire to be free from samsara and have total realization. At this point we can say we are following the Dharma correctly and are on a perfect path that will lead to perfect realization.

།ཉན་དང་སེམས་དང་ཁ་ཏོན་བྱེད་པ་ནའང་།
།རང་རྒྱུད་ཐར་པའི་དོན་དུ་དེ་བརྩམ་ཞིང་།
།འབྲི་དང་ཀློག་དང་འཛིན་དང་འཆད་པ་ནའང་།
།ཐར་པ་ཁོ་ན་འདོད་པས་བརྩམ་པར་བྱ།

When you listen to teachings, reflect on them, or recite
them aloud,
Do so for the sake of liberating your mind.
When you write, read, memorize, or explain,
Do so only out of desire for liberation.

Whatever we do that is related to Dharma practice – listening to teachings, reflecting on their meaning, chanting and doing *sadhana*[23] practices, and so on – we should always remember that we are doing these things in order to have total realization. This is how we can be sure that our practice always goes in the right direction.

།སྒོམ་དང་ལྟ་དང་སྤྱོད་པར་བྱེད་པ་ནའང་།
།ཐར་པ་ཁོ་ནའི་སེམས་དང་མ་བྲལ་བས།
།ངེས་འབྱུང་སྐྱོ་ཤས་དྲག་པོས་འབད་པར་བྱ།
།སྙིང་པོའི་མན་ངག་འདི་ལས་གོང་ན་མེད།

When you apply the meditation, view, and conduct,
Strive with intense disillusionment and renunciation
By never separating from this single-minded focus upon
liberation.

23 Literally "method of accomplishment." The practice relating to a particular deity in the Vajrayana system, involving the recitation of a liturgy and performance of ritual actions.

There is nothing higher than this,
  the heart of quintessential instructions.

In the same way, whether we are meditating, studying in order to understand the correct point of view, or trying to integrate our knowledge of the view with our behavior, we should do these things only for the purpose of being on the path and having total realization. If we are able to practice with this awareness, there is no better method for being in the essence of the teachings.

།ཟ་ཉལ་འགྲོ་འདུག་སྨྲ་བརྗོད་བསམ་ལ་སོགས།
།མདོར་ན་བྱ་བ་གང་དང་གང་བྱེད་ཀྱང་།
།ཐར་པ་འདོད་པའི་བློ་དང་མ་བྲལ་བས།
།སྐྱོ་ཤས་བསྐྱེད་དེ་སེམས་རྒྱུད་གདུལ་བར་བྱ།
།འདི་ནི་དམ་ཆོས་ལམ་དུ་འགྲོ་བའི་གནད།

When you eat, sleep, walk, sit, speak, think –
In short, in each and every thing you do –
Arouse disillusionment [toward samsara]
  and tame your mind
By never being without the desire for liberation.
This is the vital point for applying the sacred Dharma
  as a path.

Finally, even when we engage in ordinary activities like eating, sleeping, thinking, and so on, we should do these things for the sole purpose of being on the path and having total realization. This way of reeducating ourselves to always remain present and not be distracted is indispensable if we want our Dharma practice to become a path to liberation.

Longchenpa also explains here that having the desire for liberation helps us cultivate sadness about samsara, which means it is related to the principle of compassion. For example, having the intention to liberate ourselves means we recognize that it is actually possible to do so – we can enter this path, apply these teachings, and be in the state of real knowledge. We can feel happy because sooner or later we will have total realization. But how many sentient beings are totally ignorant of all this? Even if we just consider human beings, how many people have no interest in the Dharma? How many have not entered the path? If we take others into account in this way, of course we can have infinite compassion; there is no need to speak much about it or generate some artificial feeling, but just having this awareness causes real compassion to arise naturally.

For this reason, some Mahayana practitioners train in maintaining this awareness all the time, and their compassion increases day by day. For example, I once saw a video of His Holiness the Dalai Lama giving a teaching, and when he said, "There are infinite sentient beings," he suddenly started to cry. He cried for a little while and then continued with his explanation. This is an indication that his compassion is something real, something alive, and this is what Longchenpa refers to here when he speaks of cultivating deep sadness about samsara.

This way of taming our minds is very important for leading our practice in the right direction, particularly if we want to be Mahayana practitioners. At first, it is usually not so easy to reeducate our minds, because, like wild horses, we are always distracted. For this reason, there are many methods taught for the specific purpose of taming our minds a little before we go ahead with our meditation practice. So now we have a more detailed explanation of this principle.

Taking the Path of Mahayana

།ཁྱད་པར་ཐེག་ཆེན་ལམ་དུ་འགྲོ་བྱེད་པ།
།དགེ་བ་གང་བྱེད་གཞན་དོན་དམིགས་པ་སྟེ།
།སྙིང་རྗེས་སེམས་བསྐྱེད་སྨོན་བསྔོ་ཡི་རང་ཞིང་།
།སེམས་ཅན་དོན་ཕྱིར་ཡོངས་སུ་བསྒྲུབ་པའོ།

In particular, to take the Mahayana Dharma as your path,
Every act of virtue is done with the benefit of others
in mind.
Through compassion, you arouse *bodhichitta,*
make aspirations and dedications, and rejoice,
And strive wholeheartedly to accomplish the benefit
of beings.

When we apply the Mahayana principle, any virtuous activity we do is for the benefit of others, not for ourselves, and when we notice we have a selfish motive for doing something, we get rid of that kind of thinking and instead cultivate a good intention. Finally, after we have done a virtuous action, we always dedicate the merit we have accumulated for the benefit of sentient beings.

Also, when we see somebody else benefiting others, rather than feeling jealous of their virtuous behavior we think to ourselves, "How nice that this person is doing some good and helping others." In fact, by rejoicing in this way we accumulate the same merit as if we had done the action ourselves, so if we are serious about accumulating merit, this way of rejoicing in other people's virtuous behavior is particularly important.

།འདི་ལྟར་འགྲོ་ཀུན་བདག་གི་ཕ་དང་མ།
།གཉེན་དང་རྩ་ལག་ཕན་གདགས་ཞིང་ཡིན་ལ།
།བདག་ཀྱང་གཞན་དོན་བྱང་ཆུབ་སེམས་བསྐྱེད་པས།
།འགྲོ་བའི་དོན་དུ་དགེ་བ་བསྒྲུབ་པར་བྱ།
།བདག་གི་དགེ་བས་འགྲོ་བ་བདེ་བར་འགྱུར།

"All these beings have been my own father
and mother,
The friends and family I have wanted to help.
So by arousing the *bodhichitta* that benefits others,
I must accomplish virtue for their sake.
May my virtue bring these beings to happiness!"

All sentient beings have transmigrated infinite times, so in the course of these lifetimes they have all been our fathers, mothers, and other family relations. In our present life, we love our parents and our family and consider their happiness to be very important. If we consider that all beings have been our parents, our intention for benefiting others will become less limited. We will feel that we must do our best to help all these beings, and will dedicate whatever virtue we accumulate to their benefit.

།དེ་ཀུན་སྡུག་བསྔལ་བདག་ལ་སྨིན་པ་དང་།
།བདག་གི་དགེ་བ་འགྲོ་ལ་སྨིན་གྱུར་ཏེ།
།ལུས་ཅན་ཐམས་ཅད་སངས་རྒྱས་ཐོབ་པར་ཤོག
།སྙམ་དུ་ཚད་མེད་སྙིང་རྗེའི་སེམས་བསྐྱེད་སྦྱངས།

"May all their sufferings ripen in me.
May my virtues ripen in them.

And may all embodied beings attain buddhahood!"
Thinking this, train in arousing
immeasurably compassionate *bodhichitta*.

This verse describes a practice called *tonglen*[24] that is widely diffused throughout the Mahayana tradition. In this practice, we offer all our good conditions and happiness to others and take upon ourselves all their problems and suffering. Ordinary people cannot actually do this on the physical level, and for this reason we consider *tonglen* to be a kind of mind training. But even so, you should not think, "I want to do this practice to train my mind, but I will not be happy if the suffering and illness of others really does come to me." If you feel this way, *tonglen* will have no benefit, even as a mind training. So you must free yourself from this kind of thinking before you try to practice *tonglen*.

The Mahayana tradition is also called the Bodhisattvayana, the Vehicle of the Bodhisattvas. *Bodhi* means awakening, and *sattva* is a person of great courage. In the *Bodhicharyavatara*,[25] for example, Shantideva says, "Whatever happens, I will not let it disturb my peace of mind." If you do not have this attitude and are afraid of taking on the suffering of others, this means you lack the basic capacity to engage in *tonglen* practice.

If we want to develop this capacity, the *Bodhicharyavatara* contains rich teachings on how to gradually go beyond our ego and eventually change ourselves completely. Normally we view ourselves as more important than others, so the first step is to train in viewing ourselves and others as of equal importance, and to do this until we actually have

24 Literally "giving and taking."

25 *The Way of the Bodhisattva*. A renowned Mahayana text composed in the seventh century by Shantideva.

that experience. After this, we train in exchanging our own position with that of others, which is the principle of *tonglen*. Finally, we train so that we feel that others are more important than ourselves, at which point we will have courage such that even if we do become ill we will not be upset by it.

There was once a great Sakya master named Rongtön Sheja Kunrig (1367–1449). One day, when he was giving teachings on the *Prajnaparamita Sutra* and all his students were gathered around listening, a dog approached them and somebody threw a rock and hit this dog. At that moment, Rongtön cried out in pain and was unable to continue his teaching. When he asked some students to massage his side and they removed his shirt, they saw that he had in fact been hit by a stone and some of his ribs were broken. This means his practice of *tonglen* had become something real. So if you are afraid or uninterested in developing this kind of capacity, it is better to just leave *tonglen* practice aside and do another practice instead; to practice *tonglen* seriously is not so easy.

In any case, Longchenpa's instruction here is to train with the intention to receive all sentient beings' suffering, and to have them receive all our virtues and good deeds; finally we wish for all beings to become enlightened. Thinking in this way, we should cultivate *bodhichitta* and increase our compassion.

།དགེ་བ་གང་རྣམས་སྦྱོར་བ་སེམས་བསྐྱེད་དང་།
།དངོས་གཞི་མི་དམིགས་རྗེས་ལ་བསྔོ་བ་བྱ།

Whatever virtue you perform,
begin by arousing *bodhichitta*,
Perform the act itself without conceptual fixation,
and conclude by dedicating the merit.

There are three elements that should never be absent when we do any kind of practice. We call these the three sacred principles. The first of these is to begin our practice by taking refuge and cultivating *bodhichitta.* These two attitudes are indispensable. Refuge means recognizing we are on a path in order to have total realization. *Bodhichitta* means we are on this path in order to benefit all sentient beings. This prevents us from doing our practice with an egotistical motivation.

As for the second sacred principle, on the Sutrayana level, it means we always govern our practice with the knowledge of emptiness, so that even if what we are doing feels real and concrete, we always recognize that it is unreal, like an illusion. On the level of Dzogchen, it means we simply integrate everything in the self-perfected state of Dzogchen.[26]

The third sacred principle is to dedicate all the merit we have accumulated from practicing in this way to all sentient beings, so that our merit can become a cause for their liberation.

At this point, I would like to explain a little about refuge and *bodhichitta,* because many people do not understand the real sense of these attitudes, and instead of making progress on the path, they allow concepts and traditions to make them more conditioned than they were before. We are practicing in order to have total realization, which means going beyond all our illusions or limitations and entering into our real nature. We are not practicing in order to support a particular tradition.

Many people think that taking refuge means going to a teacher, reciting some verses, taking refuge vows, and then receiving a new Dharma name. They think that until this moment they were not Buddhist but now they are Buddhist. Sometimes they even receive a kind of certificate or passport from the lama, and they are even more satisfied, thinking, "Now I have a refuge passport, so I am really Buddhist!"

---

26 This integration in the self-perfected state is contemplation.

Such people are completely ignorant of the real sense of refuge. In fact, participating in this kind of ceremony changes nothing. If your name is Maria, and then you do a refuge ceremony and receive the name Tara, you might feel you have renounced your old identity, but you have not. You can tell your friends and family to call you Tara, that if they write you a letter they should address it to Tara, but this is only fantasy: your body, your speech, your mind – everything is the same Maria it was before.

But this is okay, because taking refuge does not mean we should change something. Taking refuge means knowing we are on a path. If we are applying Buddha's teachings in our life, that alone means we have taken refuge in those teachings. Buddha never said, "To follow my teachings you should become Buddhist." Buddha taught us how to discover our real nature, and our real nature is not called Buddhist, nor is it called anything else.

If you were an ordinary person with an ordinary name, and then you become a Dharma practitioner, you can consider that your ordinary name has now become your Dharma name. You can be satisfied and live with that name instead of creating more illusions, because creating illusions does not help at all. So it is very important for us to understand that following a path has nothing to do with names. In fact, even if you are called Buddha, if you do not have knowledge and understanding of your real nature it is totally meaningless. When I was young there was a local butcher named Sangye, which means Buddha in Tibetan. This man was named Buddha but he spent his whole life killing animals for money. So you see how useful a name really is.

Taking refuge also does not depend on receiving vows. People who think this way are conditioned by the Hinayana system, in which taking vows to control our body, speech, and mind is considered highly important. It is true that the principle of refuge comes originally from the Hinayana system, and it is also true that the Hinayana's emphasis on taking vows is useful for people who can only abandon negative actions by placing restrictions on themselves. But if you have a higher capacity, you can control yourself with your own presence and awareness. This is the principle of the Mahayana teachings. In this case, there is no need to be conditioned by the Hinayana style by emphasizing the taking of vows; instead, you can take refuge through presence and awareness.

This is something we really must understand, because it is actually the fundamental difference between the Hinayana and Mahayana systems. Some people think the main difference between Hinayana and Mahayana is that Hinayana practitioners have no compassion, but this kind of explanation is not at all correct. In fact, Hinayana practitioners can have extraordinarily great compassion. Arhats can directly see all the suffering of transmigration, so seeing the suffering of all sentient beings, of course they can have infinite compassion. Compared to ordinary beings like ourselves, even if we are followers of the Mahayana system, the compassion of arhats like Shariputra or Maudgalyayana is inconceivably great. Even Hinayana practitioners who are still ordinary beings apply the teaching of the Four Noble Truths as the basis for their practice, so they too are very aware of suffering and can feel compassion for all beings.

The real difference between Hinayana and Mahayana is that Mahayana practitioners can govern themselves through presence and awareness, while Hinayana practitioners govern themselves by restricting their behavior with rules and vows. Governing ourselves with awareness means we observe our intention and, if it is selfish or negative, we replace it with a good intention. Then we observe our situation and try to discover what kind of action would best correspond to our good intention. For this reason, Mahayana practitioners are much less limited and more free to help others according to the particular circumstances.

If we have the capacity to work this way, it is much more useful than taking any number of vows. When you take a vow, you have a rule that you must follow, and rules are always relative, which means they can only correspond to a limited number of situations. But the kinds of situations we can find ourselves in are limitless, so there is no vow that could correspond perfectly to every situation. If we are Mahayana practitioners and see that doing a particular action would seriously benefit others, and we have that intention, then even if it does not correspond to our vows, we can do it. A Hinayana practitioner can never work that way. That is why Mahayana is called the "greater vehicle": it is not that Mahayana is better, only more free.

In fact, Mahayana is not necessarily better or more important at all. For people who do not have the capacity to govern themselves through awareness, Hinayana is much more important than Mahayana. This is why Buddha gave the Hinayana teachings before anything else. So we must not reject the Hinayana or think it is inferior. For example, maybe we want to stop smoking cigarettes, and we try many times but never succeed. In this case, what can we do? We can take a vow: we go in front of a stupa or we go to our teacher and vow that we will not smoke cigarettes anymore. Since we consider our teacher to be a person we could never break a promise to, we can finally overcome our situation.

Especially if we are Dzogchen practitioners, we do not reject any level of the teachings, but apply them without limitations, according to our circumstances and our capacity. This does not mean we have to study everything in great detail. Even if we wanted to do this, and even if we spent our entire life trying, we would never have enough time. So instead, we should try to go to the essence, to discover the main principles of the different kinds of teachings and apply them in our practice.

For example, Atisha explained that the essence of Hinayana is to not create problems for others: that is, to control our body, speech, and mind to not commit any negative actions.[27] Then he explained that the essence of Mahayana is to always be ready to help others. If we have the capacity to work according to circumstances with our intention and awareness, not only do we control ourselves to avoid creating problems, but if someone needs help and there is something useful we can do for them, we are always ready to do it. Finally, he explained that the essence of Vajrayana is to always train in having pure vision. The cause of all our negative emotions and actions is our impure dualistic vision, so if we can transform our impure vision into pure vision, there is no way for any kind of problem or negativity to arise. This is what it means to go to the essence of the different levels of teachings. If we have this kind of understanding, all teachings can be useful.

།དེ་ཡང་འཁོར་གསུམ་ཡོངས་སུ་དག་པ་ནི།
།སྦྱང་བྱ་སྦྱོང་བྱེད་ཡོངས་སུ་སྦྱང་བ་པོ།
།སྒྱུ་འདྲ་མེད་ལ་སྣང་ཙམ་སྤྲུལ་པ་བཞིན།
།རང་བཞིན་དག་པས་གཞན་གྱི་དོན་ཕྱིར་བསྔོ།

The utterly pure three spheres –
The object of training, the act of training, and the one
who wholeheartedly applies this training –
Are nonexistent, like illusions; they are mere appearances,
like forms conjured by magic.
By means of this natural purity,
dedicate your merit to the benefit of others.

Whatever action we do, there are always three considerations: "*I* am doing this; I am doing this *for this person*; I am *doing this action* for them."

27 See Geshe Sonam Rinchen, *Atisha's Lamp to the Path of Enlightenment*, 38.

So these three aspects should always be pure, which means to not be conditioned by the interest of our ego. For example, maybe we give something to a person, but actually our thought is, "If I give something to this person today, tomorrow he will do something that benefits me." That means we are only trying to benefit ourselves, not the other person. So that is not good: we must be careful not to mix our practice of generosity with any kind of selfish motivation. When we do something for someone, we should do it simply because that person is in need. For example, if someone has no food and we have some food, we should give them some of our food with this pure motivation.

Also, whenever we do something like this, we should have the knowledge that these three aspects are not something concrete but are just like magical illusions. If we make an offering, we should know that we are making an illusory offering in order to produce an equally illusory and unreal result.

Because we are living in a state of dualistic vision, in a state of illusion, on the relative level we do need to make offerings to accumulate merit and receive obtainments. But we must always maintain an awareness that all of this is unreal.

།མོས་པ་རྒྱལ་དང་རྒྱལ་བའི་ཆོས་རྣམས་དང་།
།རྒྱལ་སྲས་དམ་པ་རྣམས་དང་བསོད་ནམས་ཞིང་།
།མ་ལུས་ཀུན་ལ་རབ་ཏུ་དད་པ་སྟེ།
།རང་དོན་གཉིས་དོན་གཞན་དོན་མོས་པ་ལས།
།བསྟོད་དང་བཀུར་དང་བསྔགས་པ་དཔེ་མེད་ཐོབ།

Aspiration means that, with total faith in the conquerors,
their teachings,
Their sublime children [the bodhisattvas],
and all other fields of merit,

You aspire to your own benefit, the twofold benefit,
and the benefit of others.
From this you gain praise, honor, and veneration
beyond compare.

Fully realized beings, the teachings they give, and the bodhisattvas who are applying these teachings are our main points of reference on the path. We call them the fields of merit because when we have confidence and faith in them and show respect to them out of devotion and the wish to benefit ourselves and others, this action accumulates great merit, which causes us to meet with all beneficial and wonderful circumstances.

།ཡི་རང་རྒྱལ་དང་དེ་སྲས་འགྲོ་ཀུན་དང་།
།དགེ་བ་ཀུན་ལ་དགའ་བ་སྒོམ་པ་སྟེ།
།འདི་ནི་བསོད་ནམས་ཕུང་པོ་དཔག་ཏུ་མེད།
།ཚད་མེད་ཆེན་པོར་བསྒྱུར་བའི་ཐབས་མཆོག་ཡིན།
།སྨོན་ལམ་རྣམ་དག་འགྲོ་བའི་དོན་ཕྱིར་གདབ།
།སྤྱོད་ཡུལ་དག་པའི་མན་ངག་བསྒོམ་པར་བྱ།

Rejoicing means cultivating joy toward every virtue
Of the conquerors, their children, and all beings.
It is the supreme method that transforms
Boundless heaps of merit into a great infinitude.
Make prayers of total purity to fulfill the purpose of others;
Apply the essential instructions on the purity
of the field of perception.

When we observe someone doing something positive and, instead of feeling jealous, we feel joy and satisfaction, we accumulate merit along with the one who is actually performing the act. So this is a way to accumulate infinite merit. Other things we can do on the mental level to accumulate merit include making invocations and aspirations and training in maintaining pure vision. When we have pure vision, any kind of action we perform is always a cause for the accumulation of merit.

།ཐ་མལ་ཕྱོགས་སུ་སྐད་ཅིག་མ་ཡེངས་པར།
།སྒོ་གསུམ་དགེ་བ་གཞན་དོན་སྙིང་པོར་བྱ།
།རང་རྒྱུད་བཏུལ་ནས་ལྷག་པའི་སེམས་བསྐྱེད་ལྡན།
།ཆོས་གང་ལམ་དུ་འགྲོ་ཞེས་བྱ་བ་ལགས།

Without becoming distracted by ordinary concerns
        for even a single moment,
Practice virtue with your three gates
        as the essence of benefit for others.
Having tamed your own mind, imbue it with
        the extraordinary intention [of *bodhichitta*]:
This is what is meant by making whatever Dharma
        [you apply]into a path.

So we must do our best not to be distracted in an ordinary way, but instead to always direct our three gates of body, voice, and mind to the path and work for the benefit of all sentient beings.

In these ways we reeducate our minds and cultivate *bodhichitta* more and more, and this is how we can be sure that we are always going in the right direction and that our path corresponds to the real sense of the Dharma.

།དེ་ལྟར་དོན་ཟབ་ངོ་མཚར་རྫ་སྨྲའི་དབྱངས།
།ཟབ་ཅིང་རྒྱ་ཆེའི་ང་རོ་སྙན་གྲགས་པ།

།མ་རིག་གཉིད་སྨྱོས་འགྲོ་ཀུན་རབ་སད་དེ།
།ཞི་བའི་དགའ་སྟོན་རྒྱ་ཆེར་མཐོང་བར་ཤོག།

May the music of this wondrous drum of the profound
meaning,
With its eminent roar, profound and vast,
Fully awaken all beings from the drunken sleep
of ignorance
To behold the vast festival of peace.

This teaching is just like a beautiful sound that awakens all people who are sleeping in a state of ignorance, leading them to the path of peace where they can obtain and enjoy the state of realization.

།ཆོས་བཞི་རིན་པོ་ཆེའི་ཕྲེང་བ་ལས།
།ཆོས་ལམ་དུ་འགྲོ་བའི་རབས་ཏེ་གཉིས་པའོ།

From *The Precious Mala of the Four Dharmas*, this is the second teaching, on applying the Dharma as a path.

So this is the second teaching, on how to make sure we are going in the right direction with the Dharma we have learned. We know it is not sufficient to remain on the level of intellectual knowledge, to learn about the Dharma but never directly apply that knowledge to our own situation. Intellectual knowledge may be useful if you want to write a book or talk about the Dharma, because somebody with a lot of intellectual knowledge will certainly have many intelligent things to say. But this kind of knowledge does not bring us closer to realization. So we must always go to the essence of the teachings, and make this something concrete in our experience.

The Third Dharma:
Clearing Away Illusion on the Path

EVEN IF WE HAVE turned our minds to the Dharma and have taken it as our path, as long as we retain our dualistic karmic vision we will still be living in a state of illusion. So we need to recognize that this dualistic vision is something unreal, and with this knowledge we can fully liberate ourselves and enter into our real nature. This is the subject of the third Dharma.

།དེ་ནས་ལམ་གྱི་འཁྲུལ་པ་སེལ་བ་ཡང་།
།ཐུན་མོང་ཁྱད་པར་བླ་ན་མེད་པ་ལས།

Then, there are common, special, and unsurpassed ways
To clear away illusion on the path.

We can become liberated by applying the common Sutra path of renunciation, the special Vajrayana path of transformation, and also the supreme Dzogchen path of self-liberation – these are called the three paths of liberation. This explanation does not exist in the Sutra teachings or in the more general Vajrayana; it is a very special explanation that we can find only in the Dzogchen teachings.

We can understand the three paths of liberation in terms of our three dimensions of existence, our three gates of body, speech, and mind. In the real sense, all methods and teachings relate to these three dimensions of our existence, and all paths correspond to these three. The path of renunciation corresponds mainly to our physical dimension, the path of transformation to our level of speech, and the path of self-liberation to our mental level. So now we will explain these paths one by one.

The Path of Renunciation

།དང་པོ་ཐུན་མོང་ཐེག་པའི་ལམ་ཆེན་གང་།
།ཚད་མེད་སེམས་བསྐྱེད་སྨོན་ལམ་སྙིང་རྗེའི་བདག
།ཐབས་ཆེན་སྤྱོད་པས་འཁྲུལ་པ་སེལ་བ་སྟེ།
།སྟོང་ཉིད་སྙིང་རྗེའི་སྙིང་པོ་དང་ལྡན་ཞིང་།
།རང་གཞན་དོན་གཉིས་ཀུན་ཏུ་སྒྲུབ་པ་ན།
།ཆོས་ཁམས་དགེ་བ་འདུས་མ་བྱས་པ་ཡི།
།གློ་བུར་དྲི་མ་རབ་ཏུ་སྦྱངས་པའི་ཕྱིར།
།ཚོགས་དང་སྦྱོར་མཐོང་སྒོམ་པའི་ལམ་བཞི་རུ།
།བྱང་ཆུབ་ཕྱོགས་ཆོས་སུམ་ཅུ་བདུན་བསྒོམ་ཞིང་།
།དག་པའི་ལྟ་བ་སྟོང་ཉིད་བཅུ་དྲུག་དང་།
།སྐྱོན་མེད་སྤྱོད་པ་ཕ་རོལ་ཕྱིན་དྲུག་རྫོགས།

First, on the general path of the Mahayana,
As a practitioner of immeasurable *bodhichitta*,
aspiration prayers, and compassion,
You clear away illusion by means of extraordinary
conduct:
When you are endowed with the essence
of emptiness and compassion

And work continuously to accomplish the twofold benefit
of self and other,
To thoroughly cleanse the temporary stains
From the virtuous and unconditioned nature
of phenomena,
You cultivate the thirty-seven factors of enlightenment
As you traverse the paths of accumulation, application,
seeing, and meditation,
Perfecting the authentic view of the sixteen emptinesses
And the faultless conduct of the six *paramitas.*

We begin with the more general teaching, the Sutrayana path of renunciation. As we know, this includes both the Hinayana and Mahayana teachings, but here Longchenpa explains it mainly according to the Mahayana system. The principle of the Mahayana teaching is the cultivation of *bodhichitta,* of which there are two kinds: relative *bodhichitta* and absolute *bodhichitta.*

There are also two aspects of relative *bodhichitta.* First, we have the *bodhichitta* of intention, which means cultivating the desire to have realization for the benefit of all beings. This is like having the wish to travel, because before we go anywhere, we must begin with that desire, that intention to travel. Then, the *bodhichitta* of application means that rather than just having the thought, we now actually do something: we do practices that can serve as a path to total realization, and we apply actions that benefit others. So this is like actually walking or driving to get where we want to go.

Absolute *bodhichitta* means the knowledge of ultimate truth, the real condition of emptiness. When we have direct knowledge of emptiness, our compassion increases infinitely, and it is not artificial but real compassion. Prior to this, we are thinking and trying deliberately to cultivate compassion, so it is always a bit artificial. But when we have real knowledge of emptiness, we no longer have this problem.

So we say that the real nature of the state of emptiness is compassion. In the real sense, this means that within our knowledge or experience of emptiness, all aspects of manifestation and movement are related to the principle of compassion. This means that compassion is not only important, but is also part of our real potentiality. So if we are missing compassion, our knowledge of emptiness has no value. Although we can find rich explanations of this principle in Vajrayana, and particularly in the Dzogchen teachings, this knowledge can already be found in the Mahayana.

The second part of this verse is especially characteristic of the teachings and explanations found in the Mahayana sutras, according to which we apply five stages, or paths, one by one to eliminate all our obstacles and negative potentialities. These are called the paths of accumulation, of application, of seeing, of meditation, and finally, the path of no more learning. Each of these paths, except for the path of no more learning, also includes individual levels that we gradually go through. The sutras contain explanations of these levels that go into great detail, such as describing which quality we obtain on each level and what kind of practice we should do to obtain it. In total, there are thirty-seven kinds of practices, called the thirty-seven factors of enlightenment, that we develop as we progress through these different stages.[28]

The first, the path of accumulation, has a lower, medium, and higher level, related to different stages of experience in our practice. From the time we enter the lowest level on this path of accumulation, we are already considered to be on the bodhisattva path, but at this

28 For a detailed explanation of this topic, see Jamgön Kongtrul Lodrö Thaye, *The Treasury of Knowledge, Books Nine and Ten.*

point we are still completely in samsara with no guarantee that we will achieve liberation.

Next come four levels on the path of application, called warmth, summit, patience, and supreme Dharma. While we are on the stages of warmth and summit, the possibility of falling into dualistic vision and samsara is still present. But when we arrive at the level of patience, it is finally guaranteed that we will no longer fall into our ordinary condition of samsara.

The third path is the path of seeing. This is the point when we can have real knowledge of absolute truth. If we wish to study this in greater detail, the sutras explain sixteen kinds of emptiness: outer emptiness, inner emptiness, empty emptiness, great emptiness, emptiness of the ultimate truth, emptiness of conditioned dharmas, and so forth.[29] There are also explanations of many different levels included on this path of seeing, but the most important thing to understand is that on this path we finally have direct knowledge of the real condition of emptiness beyond ordinary intellectual understanding.

Then, on the fourth path, the path of meditation, we have full knowledge of how to be in the state of contemplation. This is according to the Sutrayana system; the Vajrayana and Dzogchen systems have different considerations of what qualifies the state of contemplation.

In the end, when we arrive at the path of no more learning, we finally have total realization and there is nothing more to do. Also, the mode of conduct we apply on this Mahayana path is connected to the six or ten *paramitas,* and we perfect our application of these when we complete all the levels and stages of the path.

---

29 For a detailed explanation of these sixteen emptinesses, see Chandrakirti, *Introduction to the Middle Way,* 314–21.

།གང་ཟག་ཆོས་བདག་གཉིས་པོ་མེད་རྟོགས་ནས།
།ཉོན་མོངས་གཉེན་པོའི་ཐབས་ཀྱིས་སྦྱོང་བ་ནི།
།བྱང་ཆུབ་སེམས་དཔའ་རྣམས་ཀྱི་ལམ་བཟང་སྟེ།
།སྒྱུ་མ་རྨི་ལམ་འཁྲུལ་པའི་ཚུལ་ཙམ་ལས།
།སྤང་བླང་དོན་བྱས་དགེ་སྡིག་བླང་དོར་བྱེད།
།འདོད་ཆགས་ཞེ་སྡང་གཏི་མུག་ཉོན་མོངས་ལ།
།མི་གཙང་བྱམས་དང་རྟེན་འབྲེལ་ཆུ་བོས་སྦྱོང་།

Having realized that there is no self in either beings
or phenomena,
To then train in methods that remedy the emotions
Is the excellent path of the bodhisattvas.
Though things exist in no more than the illusory manner
of a dream or a magical display,
You give meaning to rejecting and accepting
by taking up virtue and casting off vice,
And wash away the emotions of attachment, anger,
and ignorance
With the water of [meditation on] impurity, love,
and interdependence.[30]

In the Sutra teachings we find the principle of the two kinds of selflessness: the selflessness of the individual and the selflessness of phenomena. At the same time, Sutrayana is the path of renunciation, which means we want to abandon our negative emotions. So Longchenpa is

30 Meditation on impurity means to meditate on the repulsive qualities of the constituents of the human body as an antidote to sexual desire. Meditation on interdependence refers to meditation on the twelve links of interdependence as an antidote to ignorance. For detailed explanations of these meditations, see Buddhaghosa's *Visuddhimagga.*

saying here that to apply antidotes to our negative emotions while integrating with the knowledge of these two kinds of selflessness is the great path of the Mahayana.

There are many detailed explanations about the two kinds of selflessness, and also different points of view and arguments between schools. But in the real sense, the meaning of selflessness, as Buddha always explained, is that everything is unreal, that our life is just like a big dream. We can understand this intellectually if we study a little, but it will only have real value for us if we integrate this understanding in our experience. In general, we are not really in that state of knowledge. Although we talk about how everything is unreal, we are still attached to our condition on the material level; we are like parrots chanting a mantra.

Once there was a yogin who lived in a cave on a mountaintop. Every day he would go for a short walk outside his cave, and as he walked he would always chant the mantra of Avalokiteshvara, OM MANI PADME HUM. Of course, he was a practitioner so he knew what he was doing; he knew precisely the reason for chanting this mantra. But there was a parrot who also lived on the mountain, and day after day the parrot heard him chanting. One day the yogin heard someone chanting OM MANI PADME HUM outside his cave, and when he looked to see who it was, he was surprised to see this parrot walking around with its head down, looking for insects to eat, saying OM MANI PADME HUM, OM MANI PADME HUM, then finding an insect and eating it, and again going back to chanting.

This story really corresponds to the situation of ordinary people. We say the words "everything is unreal," and we even understand what they mean, but our attachments never loosen even a little. If you really know everything is unreal, there is no way to feel attachment to anything. For example, if you dream you have won the lottery, of course you feel very happy, but when you wake up, your happiness goes away. If you dream that something terrible happens, you might feel very afraid, but as soon as you wake up, your fear is gone.

In the same way, we have produced the secondary causes of experiencing the karmic vision of the human dimension, so we have this kind of karmic vision until we die. Maybe we had a very nice life, maybe a very heavy life, but when we die and enter the *bardo* of existence,[31] which is not a particular part of our human dimension but a state experienced by all sentient beings, we finally discover that, as Buddha always said, our human life was just like a dream.

Many people are miserable because they are continuously agitated and do not know what to do about it. Agitation comes from giving too much importance to things. If you have real knowledge that your life is like a dream, it is impossible to give too much importance to anything. For example, because I integrate this knowledge in my daily life, I do not become agitated. You can do this, too. That is why, when my students tell me they are agitated and ask me what they should do, I always repeat those words of Buddha, that everything is unreal.

But not giving too much importance to things does not imply that we can do whatever we want. Even though we know everything is unreal, we must always do our best to apply good actions and abandon any kind of negative behavior. Why is this? Because we are still living in our relative condition. For example, we know very well that any good or bad things that happen to us in a dream are totally unreal but until we wake up, these conditions manifest for us as real. In the same way, in our ordinary relative condition, if we are doing something

31 The intermediate state beginning when one's consciousness arises with a mental body following the death process, and ending when one takes a new physical body. For a detailed explanation, see Chögyal Namkhai Norbu, *On Birth, Life, and Death,* and *Awakening Upon Dying.*

that accumulates negative karma, this causes suffering and makes our samsaric condition heavier and heavier.

So on the relative level it is necessary for us to continue to accept and reject in this way, but at the same time we should do this with the knowledge that our relative condition is unreal. And we also continue to purify our emotions of attachment, anger, and ignorance by knowing the antidotes to each one and applying them, like washing away dirt with water.

།དམ་པའི་དོན་དུ་མ་སྐྱེས་རྣམ་དག་པས།
།འཁོར་འདས་གཉིས་མེད་སྤྲོས་དང་བྲལ་བ་སྟེ།
།བདེན་པ་གཉིས་དོན་རྟེན་ཅིང་འབྲེལ་འབྱུང་ལམ།
།མཚན་ཉིད་རྒྱུ་ཡི་ཐེག་པ་ཆེན་པོ་ལགས།

Within absolute truth, samsara and nirvana
    are unborn and totally pure,
So they are nondual and free from conceptual elaboration.
This path on which the meaning of the two truths arises in
    interdependence
Is the causal Mahayana vehicle of characteristics.

The real sense of the absolute truth, the condition of emptiness that is pure from the beginning, is beyond all concepts or considerations of samsara and nirvana as two separately existing entities. In fact, the Sutra system teaches that the two truths, absolute and relative, are interdependent, and it is through interdependence that all our phenomena of samsaric vision develop out of the ultimate condition of emptiness. So we should try to be in the knowledge of Prajnaparamita, the nonduality of the two truths. This is the supreme level of knowledge in the Sutra teachings.

The Path of Transformation

Now we arrive at the particular path of the outer and inner tantras, the Vajrayana path of transformation, related to our dimension of voice or energy. As we already know, the Vajrayana path is always related to the principle of initiation, so if we want to be Vajrayana practitioners, we need to receive initiation from a qualified teacher. Without initiation, we could try applying these methods for a thousand years, but they would have no value for us; they would bring us no closer to realization.

For this reason, we must understand that in the Vajrayana system, the teacher is more important than anything else – more important even than the deity we rely on in our practice of transformation – because the entrance to the Vajrayana path is initiation, and we receive initiation from our teacher, not from the deity. So we must understand that the essence of the Vajrayana path of transformation is always Guruyoga.

།ཁྱད་པར་ལམ་ཆེན་གསང་སྔགས་ཕྱི་ནང་སྟེ།
།བསྐྱེད་རྫོགས་ཟུང་འཇུག་ཐབས་མཆོག་དཔག་ཏུ་མེད།
།སྣ་ཚོགས་རིམ་པས་འཁྲུལ་པ་སྦྱོང་བ་སྟེ།

On the special, great path of the outer and inner
Secret Mantra,
You purify illusion in various stages
Through innumerable supreme methods
of development, completion, and their union.

The Nyingma system of nine vehicles defines three series of outer tantras and three of inner tantras. The three outer series are Kriya-, Ubhaya-, and Yogatantra, and the three inner series are Mahayoga,

Anuyoga, and Atiyoga.[32] All except for Atiyoga are methods of the Vajrayana path of transformation, while Atiyoga is the Dzogchen path of self-liberation.

In the Sarma[33] traditions, the Vajrayana teachings are divided into four series – the three series of the lower tantras, which are the same as the three outer tantras in the Nyingma tradition, and one series of higher tantras called Anuttara, or Superior Tantra.

The Anuttaratantra[34] system is quite similar to the Mahayoga system of the Nyingma tradition. In fact, there are some texts that belong to both of these systems. For example, the *Guhyasamaja Tantra* is one of the most important Anuttara tantras, and it is also an important Mahayoga tantra. This is just one of many such examples. Anuyoga and Atiyoga, however, do not exist in the Sarma schools. Practitioners from all schools have always practiced these methods, but they consider Anuyoga and Atiyoga to be part of the Nyingma tradition and not the Sarma traditions.

In any case, in general, all methods of the Vajrayana path of transformation are characterized by two stages of practice: the development stage and completion stage. By practicing these two stages, we can obtain knowledge of their union or nonduality, the state of Mahamudra.

---

32 See index for the corresponding Tibetan terms for the three outer series and three inner series. However, the three inner tantras are most commonly referred to by their original Sanskrit names.

33 The Nyingma, or Old Translation, school traces its lineage back to the first propagation of Buddhism in Tibet, in the eighth century, by Guru Padmasambhava and others. The Sarma, or New Translation, schools comprise the Sakya, Kagyüd, and Gelug schools, which trace their lineages back to the second propagation of Buddhism from India to Tibet during the eleventh to thirteenth centuries.

34 Also called Anuttarayogatantra.

།གསང་སྔགས་ཕྱི་གསུམ་དག་པ་གཙོར་བྱེད་པས།
།སྤང་བླང་རེས་འཇོག་དྲི་མ་གཉེན་པོས་སེལ།

On the three outer levels of Secret Mantra,
by mainly emphasizing purity,
You alternate between rejecting and accepting
as antidotes to clear away defilements.

In the systems of the outer tantras, we mainly apply the principle of purification by using the potentiality of mantra, visualization, and so on, to purify our condition in order to prepare ourselves to receive the wisdom of enlightened beings. We call these systems the outer tantras because in these systems we consider that we are ordinary, miserable beings in samsara, and that in front of us is an enlightened being in the form of a deity like Avalokiteshvara or Tara. In addition to keeping ourselves pure, we cultivate outward devotion to the wisdom deities, praying and making offerings to them, and so on, and in this way we can also gradually receive their wisdom.

The mode of conduct in the outer tantras is to overcome obstacles by alternating between abandoning impure actions and accepting pure actions that serve as antidotes. There are many guidelines and prohibitions we must apply on the physical level, so this kind of conduct is quite similar to the conduct taught on the Sutrayana level.

But even with this similarity, the outer tantras are always considered to be part of the path of transformation because these teachings contain knowledge of the principle of the Vajra. It is true that the methods of the outer tantras begin with many dualistic aspects and concepts, but as we progress in our practice we slowly arrive at a state of integration, and the deity dissolves into us. When we are in this state of integration with the deity, we do not need to renounce our emotions because we know that emotions are the source of all manifestations and that the five primary negative emotions and five wisdoms share the same root. Because we recognize this, we can transform the emotions instead of renouncing them. This is what we mean by the principle of the Vajra.

This potentiality of the Vajra is related to our energy level, not our physical level as in the Sutra teachings. So while the Sutra path of renunciation is transmitted by *nirmanakaya* manifestations like Buddha Shakyamuni, in general all teachings related to the potentiality of the Vajra are transmitted by *sambhogakaya* manifestations. Sometimes we say that some teachings of Kriyatantra were taught by Buddha Shakyamuni in the dimension of the *devas,* which seems similar to the way in which many Mahayana sutras were taught, but most teachings of Kriyatantra and all other teachings of the lower tantras were transmitted through *sambhogakaya* manifestations. So even though the outer tantras are not as direct a path as the inner tantras, they are still part of the Vajrayana path of transformation.

།ནང་ནི་ཟུང་འཇུག་གཉིས་མེད་ཡེ་ཤེས་ཀྱིས།
།སྤང་བྱའི་དངོས་དེ་ཐབས་ཀྱིས་ལམ་དུ་བསྒྱུར།

On the inner levels, by means of the wisdom of nondual
union,
The very things that were to be abandoned
are transformed through skillful methods into the
path itself.

The inner tantras of Mahayoga and Anuyoga are the most important teachings in the path of transformation, because while it is true that the two stages of development and completion exist in outer tantras, their methods of application in the inner tantras are much more direct.

They are called the inner tantras because in these systems we do not give as much importance to performing elaborate rituals on the material level or to limiting our behavior on the physical level, and also because the conceptualization of our relationship to wisdom deities is not as dualistic as it is in the outer tantras. Instead, we try to be in a state of nonduality of our vision and its real nature, and by being in that state, rather than rejecting everything related to our impure karmic vision, we can transform it directly into pure vision.

For example, our three root emotions are ignorance, attachment, and anger – we call these the three poisons. To transform these into their pure condition, we have practices of transformation that are connected to three kinds of deities: peaceful deities to transform the emotion of ignorance, wrathful deities to transform the emotion of anger, and joyful deities to transform the emotion of attachment into its pure aspect. In this way, not only do we not need to renounce our emotions, but we are actually using them to increase wisdom.

There is something very important that we must understand about this. In the Vajrayana teachings we say the real nature of the five negative emotions is the five wisdoms. But this never means we should remain with our ordinary anger, attachment, and so on. If you have the capacity to transform your emotions into wisdoms, when you are in a state of dualistic vision and something happens to make you angry, you can manifest as a wrathful deity like Vajrakilaya, and because your condition of energy is highly charged at that moment, your practice can feel much more alive and effective. But if you transform into Vajrakilaya, it means you are in a state of pure vision, so there is no way to remain angry. You should never think that you can transform into a wrathful deity and then fight with someone. Before, you were angry because you had ordinary dualistic vision and believed that someone was creating problems for you. But now you are transformed and are no longer in your ordinary dualistic condition. Even if there are people around you, they manifest to you as wisdom beings like *dakas* and *dakinis*. How then could you continue to think that there is someone who is creating a problem? There is no tradition that teaches us to combine dualistic vision and pure vision.

Once some people came and asked me for teachings on Vajrakilaya and Mahakala. They said they had received initiations for these practices, but they did not understand very well how to apply them. I said it would be difficult for me to help, because there are many kinds of practice connected to these deities and I did not know which of them they had received. So they tried to explain a little to make me understand, and at one point they explained that in their Mahakala practice they hold a *phurpa*[35] in their hands and visualize themselves using this *phurpa* to attack all enemies of the Dharma and all personal enemies. I said, "I am sorry, but I do not know this kind of Mahakala practice." I know many practices of Mahakala, but a practice in which you transform into Mahakala and then do these kinds of things in a state of dualistic vision is just an idea invented by ordinary people.

།བདེ་གཤེགས་སྙིང་པོའི་གཞི་དབྱིངས་དཀྱིལ་འཁོར་ལ།
།རང་སྣང་ཆོས་ཀུན་རང་སེམས་སྣང་བ་ཙམ།
།འཁྲུལ་པ་དངོས་མེད་སྟོང་གཟུགས་གསལ་སྣང་ཉིད།
།ཕུང་པོ་ཁམས་དང་སྐྱེ་མཆེད་ལ་སོགས་པ།
།རིགས་ལྔ་ལ་སོགས་དག་པར་དྲན་བྱས་ཏེ།
།བསྐྱེད་པའི་རིམ་པས་སྣང་སྲིད་དཀྱིལ་འཁོར་གཅིག
།ལུས་ལྷ་ངག་སྔགས་དྲན་རྟོག་འཕྲོ་འདུར་སྦྱོང་།
།ཐ་མར་འཁྲུལ་སྣང་སངས་རྒྱས་ཞིང་དུ་བསྒྱུར།

35 A ritual dagger used in some Vajrayana practices.

In the *sugatagarbha* mandala of the real condition of the base,
All self-manifest phenomena are merely the display of your
own mind:
They are illusory and without substance,
luminous appearances of empty form.
Having engendered the recollection of the purity of the
aggregates, elements, sense faculties, and so forth
As being the five buddha families and so forth,
By means of the development stage, the entire scope
of phenomena arises as one mandala.
Your body is purified into deity, your speech into mantra, and
thought activity into the emanation and reabsorption
[of wisdom],
Until finally illusory vision is perceived as the buddhafield.

All our conceptions of vision and phenomena manifest in the mandala of our real condition, just like appearances manifesting in a mirror. In fact, although we imagine that illusion or samsaric vision is something concrete that we have produced through our karma, it is not concrete at all; it is only what we call empty form. Even while it is apparently manifesting as form, in that moment it is already emptiness. For example, I can see a table and place objects on it, so relatively, it seems like something concrete. But its real condition is always emptiness. These aspects of emptiness and form are nondual. In the relative sense we can speak of two aspects, but in the real sense there are not two entities. This is what we mean by being in the nonduality of our quality of vision and its real nature.

So in the development stage, with this kind of knowledge or wisdom, we can transform our vision so that everything in our ordinary impure vision is transformed into a dimension of pure vision. Our aggregated physical body, our potentiality of the five elements, our sense faculties, the physical organs that are their support in our body, and all their different objects – all aspects of our experience of subject and object – are perfected in their pure aspect as deities in one unified mandala, without any concept of subject and object or dualistic vision.

By practicing pure recollection in this way, our physical level manifests as the form of the deity, our voice or energy level manifests as mantras, and all our thoughts manifest as wisdom, so that eventually all our illusory vision manifests only as a pure dimension, or buddhafield. This is the development stage.

།རྫོགས་པའི་རིམ་པས་ཐམས་ཅད་ཆོས་ཉིད་དང་།
།བསམ་གྱིས་མི་ཁྱབ་འོད་གསལ་དབྱིངས་ལ་འཇུག
།རྩ་དང་རླུང་དང་ཐིག་ལེའི་རྣལ་འབྱོར་གྱིས།
།རླུང་སེམས་ལས་རུང་དབྱིངས་དང་ཡེ་ཤེས་སྦྱོར།

By means of the completion stage,
    everything enters into the dimension
Of the real nature and inconceivable luminous clarity.
Through the yogas of the channels, energies,
    and essences,
Your energies and mind acquire special pliancy,[36]
    and the real condition and wisdom are unified.

36 Literally "fit for action." A reconfiguration of the energies of the individual that allows for any virtuous activity of body or mind to be performed with great ease, without fatigue, and with flawless attention. It is also sometimes associated with the acquisition of supernormal powers and extrasensory modes of perception.

Once you have developed sufficient clarity and ability by practicing the development stage in this way, you are ready to begin to practice the completion stage, which means integrating the transformation state with all dimensions of your existence. This step is necessary because, for example, if you are practicing the development stage by visualizing yourself as Kalachakra and your dimension as the mandala of Kalachakra, the clarity and presence of your visualization might be very stable, but at the same time you are always aware of your impure body and your impure dimension, and are not working directly with that part of your experience.

When you apply the completion stage, you no longer separate the pure and impure condition. You work with the channels and chakras in which your prana energy and kundalini energy move and circulate, which means you are now integrating your energy level in the transformation state. Before, you were only working with your mind to construct a visualization, but compared to the mental level, your energy level is much more closely connected to your physical level, so now it is possible to integrate all levels of your existence in the pure dimension, and it becomes something alive, something you can feel and not just imagine. When we practice in this way, all phenomena manifest in their real condition of luminosity, and we integrate in a condition of nonduality of the real nature and its qualities of wisdom.

།ཟུང་འཇུག་དབྱེར་མེད་ཕྱག་རྒྱ་ཆེན་པོའི་ལམ།
།འབྲས་བུ་གསང་སྔགས་རྡོ་རྗེ་ཐེག་པ་ལགས།

This is the path of the indivisible union of Mahamudra,
The fruitional Secret Mantra Vajra Vehicle.

Finally, when you approach the state of realization on this Vajrayana path, you enter into what is called the nonduality of the development and completion stages, and at this point you can say that you are in the state of Mahamudra. This state of the nonduality of the development and completion stages is the final goal of Vajrayana practice, and it is the original meaning of Mahamudra. There is no difference between this state of Mahamudra and the state of Dzogchen, but unlike in the Dzogchen path of self-liberation, we arrive at the state of Mahamudra by progressing gradually through the two stages of Vajrayana practice. If you want to have a more thorough understanding of Mahamudra, there is a book by Sakya Pandita that explains everything very clearly.[37]

Many people are confused about Mahamudra. For example, the Mahamudra teachings of the Kagyüd tradition comprise a special method of Mahamudra that comes from Gampopa. Many people say this is not true, and that the Mahamudra teachings given by Gampopa originally came from India. Many ancient Mahamudra teachings in fact do come from India, and they all explain Mahamudra as the final goal of the Anuttaratantra path of gradual transformation. For example, some important explanations and songs of Mahamudra come from the *mahasiddha* Saraha, who was historically the most important practitioner of the *Guhyasamaja Tantra*. We also have important Mahamudra teachings that come from the *mahasiddha* Virupa. Virupa was a practitioner of the *Hevajra Tantra*, and he taught Mahamudra as the final goal of that practice. Many of the most important teachings of the Kagyüd school come from Tilopa, whose teachings are connected to the *Chakrasamvara Tantra*. So all of these teachers presented Mahamudra as the final goal of Anuttaratantra practice.

---

37 See Sakya Pandita in bibliography.

But Gampopa taught Mahamudra in a very different way, as a method called the Four Yogas of Mahamudra. He was a very important student of Milarepa, and a great practitioner of Anuttaratantra, but he was also an expert in the method of Dzogchen Semde; he integrated these Dzogchen teachings with his knowledge of Mahamudra, and that is the way he taught. In fact, his teaching on the Four Yogas is connected to a very ancient method of Dzogchen Semde called the Four Contemplations.[38] Gampopa became something like the main source of the entire Kagyüd lineage, so of course his Mahamudra teachings were widely diffused throughout all branches of the Kagyüd tradition. There are also many Nyingma lineages that practice Dzogchen Semde and Gampopa's Mahamudra teachings together. For example, Adzom Drugpa wrote a nice book combining these two systems, explaining everything in great detail. But there is not a single Indian text translated from Sanskrit that explains this Mahamudra system of the Four Yogas.

When I explain this fact, some people get upset and deny that it is true. But there is no reason to be upset about this. You do not need to have the idea that whatever comes from India is very sacred and perfect, and whatever comes from Tibet is not important. This is only a Tibetan idea. There is a story someone made up and added to the biography of Milarepa that illustrates of this way of thinking. In this story, Pha Tampa Sangye (eleventh century) and Milarepa meet in person and decide to have a competition to see who has greater mastery of *kumbhaka*.[39] Pha Tampa Sangye performs his *kumbhaka* and sits on the tip of a blade of grass, and this blade of grass remains perfectly straight.

38 The Four Yogas of Mahamudra are single-pointed state, nonelaboration, single taste, and nonmeditation. The Four Contemplations of Dzogchen Semde are calm state, nonmovement, equality, and self-perfection.

39 Literally "vase-like breathing." A yogic technique often associated with the completion stage of Anuttaratantra. See Chögyal Namkhai Norbu, *Yantra Yoga*.

Then Milarepa does the same thing, but his blade of grass bends just a little. Then Pha Tampa says, "Oh, Milarepa! Between you and I there is no difference in realization or capacity. Your blade of grass only bends a little because you took birth in Tibet." I feel that this is really a stupid idea. We consider that India is a sacred place because Buddha and many of his students lived there, so now India is blessed by Buddha's wisdom. But how can the wisdom of Buddha be limited by distance? Wisdom limited by distance is not the wisdom of an enlightened being.

In any case, the final goal of the gradual path of transformation is generally called Mahamudra. However, in the Anuyoga system, the final goal is called Dzogchen. In the real sense, there is no difference between the state of Mahamudra and the state of Dzogchen, but we say the goal of Anuyoga is the state of Dzogchen because in the Anuyoga system, even though we are using the method of transformation, we also have the knowledge that our real nature is self-perfected from the beginning, just as we understand in the Dzogchen teachings. Because we have this base of knowledge, the way of applying the path in Anuyoga is also different: we can transform instantly, rather than gradually as we do in the Anuttaratantra or Mahayoga systems.

When we practice Mahayoga, we have to read many verses that describe what we should visualize step by step. As we chant these verses, we visualize all these things one by one until we have constructed the entire mandala of our pure dimension. But in Anuyoga, we do not need to work in this way. From the beginning, our real nature has its three primordial potentialities of sound, light, and rays. This means that like reflections in a mirror, whenever there is a secondary cause, anything can instantly manifest.

If I hold a *vajra* in front of a mirror, its reflection immediately manifests there. The mirror does not need to create this reflection gradually, step by step, because the mirror has the capacity to manifest instantly.

If I do not hold the *vajra* up to the mirror, nothing will manifest there, because there is no secondary cause. But as soon as that secondary cause is present, the reflection instantly manifests.

In the same way, in the Anuyoga system, when we receive an initiation from our teacher and he introduces us to the transformation state, this is the secondary cause through which our primordial potentiality of sound, light, and rays manifests as the deity in its pure dimension. So this Anuyoga system is a way of applying the knowledge of our self-perfected state to the Vajrayana path of transformation.

The Path of Self-Liberation

Now we come to the Dzogchen path of self-liberation. First we must understand what Dzogchen means. Dzogchen means our real nature, our real condition. The word Dzogchen means total perfection[40] because our real nature is primordially pure and self-perfected with all qualities from the beginning. There are many teachings, instructions, and methods for understanding and discovering this, and for integrating everything in this state. All these instructions and methods are called the Dzogchen teachings. By making a clear distinction between the state of Dzogchen and the teachings of Dzogchen, we can understand that although only a limited number of people are interested in applying the teachings of Dzogchen, the real nature of all sentient beings is always Dzogchen. Even the nature of a small ant is Dzogchen.

40 This term is more commonly rendered as Great Perfection. However, as Chögyal Namkhai Norbu explains, there is a risk of understanding "great" in its comparative sense, as something "not small." Instead, the meaning of *chen* here is all-inclusiveness beyond concepts of greater or lesser.

།བླ་མེད་ཐེག་པ་མཆོག་གསང་རྫོགས་པ་ཆེ།
།ལྷུན་གྲུབ་དབྱིངས་ལ་དངོས་སུ་སྦྱོར་བ་སྟེ།

In the unexcelled vehicle of the supreme and secret
Total Perfection,
You connect directly with your self-perfected
real condition.

The practice of Dzogchen is called Atiyoga, meaning primordial yoga or knowledge of our primordial state, because as soon as we enter this path, our teacher directly introduces us to our primordial state of Dzogchen. This state of Dzogchen is also the state of our teacher, so being in our real nature means being in the state of our teacher. From this we can see that the essence of the practice of Dzogchen is Guruyoga.

When we receive this direct introduction from our teacher, we are not working with our energy level in the same way as when we receive a Vajrayana initiation; rather, we are working with our mental level, going directly from our ordinary mind within time to its real nature beyond time and space.

We can understand how this is done through the example of a mirror. When we look at our reflection in a mirror, we know very well that the reflection is unreal. The reflection is there because the mirror has the unlimited potentiality to reflect anything according to secondary causes. So we can easily understand the difference between the reflections in the mirror and the nature of the mirror itself, which is the capacity to manifest those reflections. Although the nature of the mirror is not something we can see or touch, we can discover that its nature is to manifest reflections by seeing these reflections manifesting; the reflections have the quality of demonstrating the mirror's infinite potentiality.

In the same way, the nature of our mind has infinite potentiality to manifest visions and experiences according to secondary causes. Our ordinary mind is always related to different kinds of experiences, and in general we are conditioned by these experiences and do not know how to go beyond this conditioning. But in the real sense, these experiences manifest through the potentiality of the nature of our mind, and through these experiences we can discover our real nature beyond experiences. This is the principle of direct introduction.

In general, there are three kinds of experiences we use for this purpose: the experience of emptiness, related to the level of mind; the experience of clarity, related more to our energy or voice; and the experience of sensation or bliss, related to our physical body. These experiences are totally different from each other: the experience of bliss is not the experience of clarity, and the experience of clarity is not the experience of emptiness. This is how we experience things in our state of ordinary presence. But a practitioner of Dzogchen can also be in the state of instant presence, which means being in the nature of our mind. That state is never conditioned by any kind of experience. For example, we cannot say there is "instant presence of clarity" or "instant presence of emptiness."

Being in the state of instant presence is something like being in the nature of the mirror rather than in its reflections. The mirror has no problem with any reflection that manifests: whatever the reflection is, the mirror clearly and perfectly manifests it. This is the quality of the mirror: it is always clear, pure, and limpid, and that is all. When we are in instant presence, in the nature of mind, we are not limited or conditioned by anything that manifests, so everything that manifests self-liberates.

This is our natural state, to which our teacher directly introduces us from the very beginning of the path of Dzogchen. There are many ways of giving this direct introduction, and a teacher uses one or another depending on a particular student's condition. For example, if the student does not have much attachment to Vajrayana ritual, this introduction can be given in a very simple way. But students who are attached to the Vajrayana style will not be satisfied unless there is a ritual to perform, as there is in a Vajrayana initiation.

In an initiation, the teacher puts something on your head, and sometimes pours water on your head. There is something to drink, maybe something to eat – there are always many things to do. If we combine direct introduction with this kind of initiation, people who are attached to this system will be satisfied and feel that now they have really received something from the teacher. For example, once I was giving a Dzogchen teaching in Turin, northern Italy, and at this teaching I also gave direct introduction in a very simple way. I was satisfied and thought that maybe the people had understood something. But after the teaching, a small group of people approached me. They said they were followers of Sufism, and that in the Sufi tradition one must receive a kind of initiation, so they wanted me to give them an initiation as well. I told them that the principle of Dzogchen is direct introduction, not initiation, and I had already given them this direct introduction. Also, in that moment I had no time to give them an initiation. Then they said, "If you will not give us an initiation, at least please touch us." So I told them to come near and I touched them one by one, and then they were satisfied. This means they considered it more important for me to touch them than to give them direct introduction to their real nature. So for people like this, we can do something to make them happy, but we must understand that initiation is not the main principle in Dzogchen. If we want to be Dzogchen practitioners, what is indispensable is that we receive direct introduction.

Some people say that before receiving direct introduction we should complete what are called the preliminary practices, or ngöndro.[41] Teachers from all traditions generally consider that students should do these preliminary practices before they can learn more essential teachings. This is the traditional way in Tibet. But in the Sutra teachings, Buddha himself said that teachers should teach the Dharma according to the student's circumstances, capacity, and interest. He never said we should always work according to tradition. Of course, if we want to follow the traditional way and we have the opportunity, it is very useful. I myself completed the *ngöndro* twice, so I know its functions and benefits very well. But it is more important to look at our circumstances and then work intelligently with them.

For example, in the modern world we usually do not have time to do a traditional *ngöndro*. In Tibet, in the past, it was not as difficult, because people could live very simply, just cultivating some barley or potatoes to eat and living quietly in the countryside. But in our modern society we cannot live that way. Every month we have many bills have to pay – for electricity, water, healthcare, education for our children, and so on – so we always have to make money. This means we need to have a job, which always leaves us so busy that it is not easy to find time to practice Dharma. Because we have no time to do many complicated practices, we should concentrate instead on the essence of the teachings. This is what it means for us to work with our circumstances.

Also, as Buddha said, a teacher should work according to the capacity of the student. When teachers say it is negative to teach Dzogchen until the student has done *ngöndro*, in the real sense, this only means they are conditioned by the ordinary way of doing things in our

41 Literally "what goes before". For a detailed presentation of these practices, see Paltrul Rinpoche, The Words of My Perfect Teacher.

human society. For example, if we want to go to university, we need a high school diploma, and to get this diploma we need to go to high school. To go to high school, we need to first go to elementary school. When people who are conditioned by this kind of system see a new student, they may have the idea that this person does not yet have a high enough capacity to practice Dzogchen and should first attend elementary school. But such people do not know what capacity really means. Having the capacity to follow the Dzogchen teachings does not mean you already have some level of realization. If you understand what the teacher explains to you, and if you are interested in applying his teachings, this indicates that you have sufficient capacity.

Also, someone may be new to the Dzogchen teachings in this life, but we have all had infinite lifetimes in samsara, and in our relative condition it is not so easy to meet the Dzogchen teachings. So if a person is meeting these teachings now, it indicates that he already has a very precise connection with these teachings and their transmission, whether or not he himself has this idea.

Finally, Buddha said we should work according to the student's desire. For example, when Westerners discover that the essence of the Dzogchen teachings is to introduce and go directly into knowledge of their real nature, they want to receive and apply that kind of teaching, and when Nyingma or Kagyüd teachers come to the West, many people request them to teach Dzogchen. This indicates that they have the desire, so we must respect that as well.

Not only does this approach correspond to the teachings of Buddha Shakyamuni, but it also corresponds perfectly to the teachings of Garab Dorje, whom we consider to be the most important teacher of Dzogchen. In this epoch, Garab Dorje was the first to introduce the Dzogchen teachings in our dimension. When he was still a small child, he began to teach and transmit the Dzogchen tantras, and he lived for a long time and taught Dzogchen for many years. In the end, he manifested the rainbow body,[42] and as his final teaching, he gave three statements, as the essence of everything he had taught, to his student Manjushrimitra. So we can understand that everything in the Dzogchen teachings is related to these three statements of Garab Dorje, and we can be confident that if we work according to their principles, we will be applying the Dzogchen teachings in a perfect way.

The first statement is that we should discover our real nature through direct introduction. The second is that once we have been introduced to our real nature, we should go beyond all doubt about what is our natural state and what is not. The third statement is that when we have this knowledge in a perfect way, we should continue in that state.

If Garab Dorje had believed it was always necessary to do *ngöndro,* he would have given four statements: first do *ngöndro,* then receive the direct introduction, and so on. We cannot say that he forgot something, because Garab Dorje is a totally enlightened being and an enlightened being cannot make that kind of mistake. So when teachers criticize me for teaching Dzogchen to people who have not done *ngöndro,* I tell them to argue with Garab Dorje instead.

།གཞི་དབྱིངས་མི་འགྱུར་ནམ་མཁའ་ལྟ་བུ་ལ།
།ཡོན་ཏན་ལྷུན་གྲུབ་ཉི་ཟླ་གཟའ་སྐར་བཞིན།
།བཙལ་བ་མེད་པར་ཡེ་ནས་ལྷུན་གྲུབ་པས།
།འབད་ཅིང་རྩོལ་མེད་རང་བཞིན་མངོན་སུམ་ལམ།

In the real condition of the base, like the changeless sky,

42 The culmination of the Dzogchen path of self-liberation, in which one's physical body dissolves into the essence of the elements. Also called the body of light. See Chögyal Namkhai Norbu, *The Crystal and the Way of Light,* 158–62, and *Rainbow Body.*

All qualities are self-perfected, like the sun, moon,
and stars.
And since they are self-perfected in this way
from the beginning, with no need to be sought,
This is the path on which your real nature manifests
directly, without effort or exertion.

As we explained already, in the Dzogchen teachings we say that our real nature is the nonduality of primordial purity, or *kadag,* and self-perfection, or *lhundrub.* So here Longchenpa gives the example that our state of *kadag,* which corresponds to the condition of emptiness described in the Sutra teachings, is just like space, and our potentiality of all self-perfected qualities manifests just like the sun, moon, and infinite stars shining in that dimension.

We use this kind of explanation to help us think and understand with our intellectual minds, but our real nature does not actually have two aspects of *kadag* and *lhundrub.* Our real nature is always a unity, and this is why we say it is the nonduality of *kadag* and *lhundrub.* This type of explanation can give us some idea about our nature, but having an idea does not mean we have discovered Dzogchen. We discover Dzogchen when we work with the transmission from our teacher, apply instructions and methods, and finally get in the real knowledge of that condition. Then we can say we have real knowledge of Dzogchen.

We should distinguish well between believing something and discovering it. What we need when we follow the Dzogchen teachings is to discover, not to believe. Belief is always related to our mind, and our mind is in time and space, so we can believe one thing today, but our beliefs can always change tomorrow. We may change our beliefs a hundred thousand times, but in the real sense nothing changes for us: we are always in dualistic vision, we are always ignorant.

Our real nature is beyond mind, beyond time and space. For this reason, in the Dzogchen teachings we distinguish between our mind and the nature of our mind. Whenever we are thinking and judging, trying to intellectually understand our real nature, this is mind. When we are just being in the state of the nature of our mind, the nonduality of *kadag* and *lhundrub* beyond all limitations of thinking and judging, we are discovering our real nature and really being in that knowledge. This real nature is something that all of us have from the beginning. It is not something we need to search for, obtain, or develop by following a teacher and applying an instruction or method.

If we are applying the Sutrayana principle, it seems we are producing something through effort, because we must first go step by step through the three levels of the path of accumulation, then the four levels of the path of application, and so on. Eventually we arrive at the first *bhumi*,[43] and from there we continue step by step until we reach the tenth *bhumi*. But when we say our nature is primordially pure and self-perfected with all qualities, it means that each of us, from the very beginning, has all the qualities of the tenth *bhumi*. This is the principle of the Dzogchen teachings. As we can see, it is very different from the kind of understanding found in other teachings, but if we discover our real nature and are able to be in that knowledge, we can see very easily that this is how it really is.

For example, when I was in monastic college, I studied a very important text called the *Ornament of Clear Realization*.[44] This text explains in great detail all the qualities of the different levels of realization on

43 In the Mahayana system, the *bhumis* are the ten stages of the bodhisattva path that begin from the moment one attains direct knowledge of emptiness up to the final achievement of buddhahood.

44 The *Abhisamayalankara*, one of five scriptures revealed by Buddha Maitreya to the great Indian master Asanga.

the Hinayana and Mahayana paths. The first time I studied this text it did not seem very difficult to understand. But then I studied it a second time and it seemed more difficult than before, so I asked my teacher at the monastery what to do about it. This teacher was a Dzogchen practitioner as well as a scholar, and when I asked him about this he gave me some interesting advice. He said I should not think that this text is only describing the qualities of arhats and bodhisattvas; it is describing my own condition as well. I tried reading the text again with this in mind, but at that time I had no real understanding or knowledge of Dzogchen, so his advice did not help very much; the text seemed to have nothing to do with me.

But much later, when I was working at the University of Naples, one day I came across this text in the library, and I remembered this teacher's advice and thought it would be interesting to try reading it again. I took it home and read it when I had free time on weekends. At that time I had already received transmission and knowledge of Dzogchen, so now I could understand perfectly what my teacher had said before, and this time when I read it I could understand everything very easily.

View

།འོད་གསལ་དབྱིངས་ཀྱི་དཀྱིལ་འཁོར་འདུས་མ་བྱས།
།རང་གནས་ཆོས་སྐུ་མཉམ་པའི་དགོངས་པ་ཉིད།
།རྟོགས་པར་བྱེད་པ་གནས་ལུགས་ལྟ་བའི་མཆོག

The supreme view of the natural state brings you
to the realization
Of the state of equality of naturally abiding *dharmakaya*,
The uncompounded mandala of the real condition
of luminous clarity.

Our real condition is the *dharmakaya* dimension of natural light, which is not constructed or produced. When we discover and are able to be in this knowledge concretely, that is what we call the perfect point of view according to the Dzogchen teachings. When we speak of the *dharmakaya* or the three *kayas* in the context of the Dzogchen teachings, we need to know that the way of understanding them here is different from the way of understanding them in the Sutrayana teachings.

In the Sutrayana, the three *kayas* are only considered to be the qualities of fully enlightened beings, which manifest when they have already gone through the ten *bhumis* and arrived at the fruit of total realization. But in the Dzogchen teachings we have an explanation of the three *kayas* of the base, three *kayas* of the path, and three *kayas* of the fruit.

Base means our real nature from the beginning. Our real nature has its qualities of the three wisdoms – of essence, nature, and energy – and these are what we call the three *kayas* of the base. Then, when we are working with different methods on the path, we can have three characteristic types of experiences: experiences of emptiness, of clarity, and of sensation or bliss. These are the three *kayas* of the path. Finally, when we have total realization, our condition is the three *kayas* of the fruit, which all schools accept.

This explanation of the three *kayas* of the base, path, and fruit is something very special that exists only in the Dzogchen teachings. Some scholars believe that this explanation does not correspond to the correct view, and they try to debate and refute it, but this only indicates that they are ignorant of the real meaning of view. In general, we consider that a point of view is something we establish with our dualistic mind's faculty of logic. For example, we consider that the Gelug point of view is based on the positions established by Tsongkhapa through his logic, and that the views of other schools are based on the positions that their learned masters established using logic. All these schools continuously debate and argue with each other about which view is the correct one, and many hundreds of volumes have been written arguing these points and trying to establish that one school's view is correct.

When I was studying in monastic college, my college officially belonged to the Sakya school, so we mostly studied books and commentaries belonging to that school. I was convinced that the Sakya point of view was the perfect one, that the Gelug view was not perfect at all, and that the Kagyüd point of view was only so-so. But later, when I received direct introduction from my teacher Changchub Dorje,[45] I finally discovered what "view" really means, and saw how limited my previous understanding had been.

When we have real knowledge, which does not come from our intellect but is something we have discovered concretely in our condition, that is what we call having the correct or supreme point of view. In fact, no position established through logic can ever be the correct point of view, because logic always depends on dualistic vision, and dualistic vision is always illusion. That is why my teacher Changchub Dorje told me there is nothing to be established with logic and analysis, that we can only discover the real sense of the view by observing our own condition. He explained that a view established through logic is like a pair of eyeglasses, because even very powerful eyeglasses can only help us see the objects in front of us more clearly; we still remain in dualistic vision. But the correct point of view is like a mirror, because when we look in a mirror we see our own face. When we look in a mirror and observe ourselves a little, first we can see what kinds of limitations we have, how we are conditioned, and then we can go

45 Chögyal Namkhai Norbu's root teacher (1863–1961). See Chögyal Namkhai Norbu, *The Temple of the Great Contemplation,* for a biography of Rigdzin Changchub Dorje.

beyond those limitations. This is important, because if we remain in any kind of limitation, it is impossible to have the correct point of view.

།དག་པའི་དབྱིངས་ལ་གློ་བུར་སྒྲིབ་པའི་སྤྲིན།
།འགྲོ་སེམས་འཁྲུལ་སྣང་མེད་བཞིན་སྣང་བ་ཡིས།
།ཁམས་གསུམ་རིགས་དྲུག་བརྒྱུད་ཅིང་ཅིར་སྣང་ཡང་།
།སྣང་བའི་དུས་ན་དོན་ལ་གྲུབ་པ་མེད།
།མཁའ་དང་སྤྲིན་བཞིན་གློ་བུར་རྐྱེན་སྣང་ཙམ།

In the expanse of purity of the real condition,
A passing veil of clouds – the illusory display of beings' minds –
Appears without existing and causes them to traverse the three realms and six classes.
But however these phenomena manifest, they have no reality, even in their moment of appearing:
Like clouds in the sky, they are just a display of passing conditions.

All our illusions are just like clouds temporarily manifesting in the empty and pure dimension of space. These illusory visions do not actually exist somewhere as something real, but because of our ordinary dualistic minds, all sentient beings think these appearances are something real and concrete, so we accept and reject them, produce good and bad karma with happiness and suffering as a result, and now we have samsara: the three realms and six classes arise, and we transmigrate continuously from one to the next. So just like clouds, our karmic vision is always changing because of secondary causes and conditions, but like the space of the sky, our real nature of *dharmakaya* never changes, no matter what kind of appearances manifest for us on the relative level.

།འཁོར་བ་སྒྲོ་བཏགས་མཚན་ཉིད་ཆད་པ་སྟེ།
།མེད་བཞིན་སྣང་སྟེ་རང་གི་ངོ་བོས་སྟོང་།
།སྟོང་སྣང་དངོས་མེད་རབ་རིབ་སྐྲ་ཤད་དང་།
།རྨི་ལམ་སྒྱུ་མ་དུང་ལ་སེར་འཛིན་བཞིན།
།ཇི་ལྟར་སྣང་དུས་ཉིད་ནས་གྲུབ་མ་མྱོང་།
།གཞི་མེད་རྟེན་མེད་ཐོག་མ་དབུས་མཐའ་མེད།
།རང་བཞིན་གདོད་ནས་དག་པར་ཤེས་པར་བྱ།
།འདི་ལྟར་སྣང་སྲིད་སྣོད་བཅུད་ཆོས་རྣམས་ལ།
།གཟུང་བའི་ཡུལ་མེད་སྤྲུལ་པ་མིག་ཡོར་བཞིན།
།འཛིན་པའི་སེམས་མེད་བར་སྣང་དག་པ་འདྲ།
།གཟུང་འཛིན་གཉིས་མེད་འཁོར་བ་ཡོད་མ་མྱོང་།

Samsara is a false premise without the marks of existence.
Appearing without existing, it is empty of essence.
Its empty appearances are substanceless,
like strands of hair seen by diseased eyes,
Like a dream, a magical display, or a white conch
seen as yellow.
So from their very moment of appearing, in whatever ways
they have, these visions have never been present at all.
Without basis, without support, without beginning,
middle, or end,
Know that by nature [samsara] is pure from the beginning.
Within the entire scope of phenomena
of worlds and beings,
Like conjured forms or hallucinations,
there are no objects to grasp;
And like pure empty space there is no mind to grasp them.
And without these two – grasper and grasped –
samsara has never existed.

We have this experience of transmigration because this is what appears to be happening in our condition of dualistic vision through the secondary causes of our karma and emotions. But in the real sense, there is no cycle of samsara: even as these visions are appearing to us, their nature is already emptiness, so what we call transmigration is only a name without any kind of logic. But even though samsara has no real existence, our experience of samsara will continue to manifest as long as we have the secondary causes of dualistic vision and emotions.

For example, a person who has an illness connected to the humor of phlegm[46] can have visions that make him see strands of hair everywhere. Or if he has an illness connected to bile humor, things that are white will appear to be yellow. That yellow color is not actually there – he is only seeing it due to the secondary cause of his illness. In the same way, whatever manifests to us appears to be solid and real, but from the first moment we see these things, there is nothing there at all: nothing has existed from the beginning, nothing exists right now, and nothing will ever exist in the future. All the phenomena in our entire universe are just like hallucinations or appearances in a magic show. Not only the objects you see, but also your self as the subject who sees them is not something you can actually find, point to, and say, "This is my mind. My mind is seeing that object." Without a subject or an object, how can we consider that there is a cycle of transmigration?

།མེད་སྣང་འཁྲུལ་པ་རང་བཞིན་ཤེས་པས་གྲོལ།
།སྤང་བླང་རྒྱུ་འབྲས་རྐྱེན་སྣང་རང་དག་པས།
།གནས་ལུགས་དོན་ལ་རྒྱུ་འབྲས་འདས་ཤེས་བྱ།

46 For a discussion of the three humors in Tibetan medicine, see Chögyal Namkhai Norbu, *On Birth, Life, and Death.*

Nonexistent illusory appearances are released
when their nature is known.
Since rejection and acceptance, cause and effect,
and conditioned appearances are themselves pure,
Understand that the natural state really is beyond cause
and effect.

When we are able to really be in the knowledge that our karmic vision has no essence, that it is only illusion, we are liberated from that condition. This means all our problems and suffering are always related to our mind and our ignorance. But in the real sense, everything is pure, including all our dualistic considerations like accepting and rejecting, cause and effect, and so on, because the real nature of everything is emptiness; none of it has ever actually existed. This is our understanding according to the Dzogchen teaching, and this is why the Dzogchen teaching is called the teaching beyond cause and effect.

But it is important not to misunderstand this. Many people hear this and think that if they follow the Dzogchen teaching they do not need to pay attention to karma. This is totally wrong. It is true that your real nature is the state of Dzogchen, and the state of Dzogchen is beyond cause and effect, so if you can remain in instant presence forever, you are beyond cause and effect. But ordinarily we are always falling into dualistic vision, and if we are in dualistic vision, how can we say that cause and effect do not exist for us? We must be careful to not have these kinds of wrong ideas.

།དེ་ཡི་ རྗེན་གཞི་རིག་པ་བྱང་ཆུབ་སེམས།
།སྨྲ་ངན་འདས་དབྱིངས་ལྷུན་གྲུབ་ཆེན་པོ་ནི།
།དོན་དམ་བདེན་པ་གདོད་ནས་དག་པ་སྟེ།
།ཐོག་མ་དང་ནི་ཐ་མ་མེད་པའི་བདག

།རང་བཞིན་འོད་གསལ་ཟབ་ཞི་སྤྲོས་དང་བྲལ།
།ཡེ་ནས་རང་གནས་ཆོས་སྐུ་དྲི་མ་མེད།
།དུས་གསུམ་འཕོ་འགྱུར་མེད་པའི་ངོ་བོར་གནས།
།འདི་ནི་གཞི་དབྱིངས་རྡོ་རྗེ་སྙིང་པོ་སྟེ།
།གང་གིས་དེ་རྟོགས་གནས་ལུགས་ལྟ་བ་ཉིད།
།སྒྲོ་སྐུར་ཞི་བ་དོན་གྱི་སྙིང་པོར་རྟོགས།

The base of all of this is *rigpa bodhichitta,*
The real condition beyond all suffering,
    the total state of self-perfection.
This is the ultimate truth, primordial purity,
The true identity without beginning or end,
Natural luminous clarity, profound, peaceful,
    and free of elaboration.
It is the primordially self-existing, stainless *dharmakaya*
That abides as the essence beyond the three times
    of transition and change.
It is the Vajra essence, the real condition of the base,
And whoever realizes it has the authentic view
    of the natural state,
The realization of the actual essence
    wherein all affirmations and denials are pacified.

Our real nature of instant presence, or *rigpa,* which we have from the beginning, is itself nirvana, the state of all enlightened beings, which the Sutrayana teachings call ultimate truth. Its nature is clear light, deep and peaceful and beyond all concepts. This is the real *dharmakaya,* so even if we are in our ordinary mind within time and space, it makes no difference because *dharmakaya* has no past, present, or future; our real nature is beyond any consideration of time and space. This is called the essence of the Vajra, and when we are in this state of knowledge, beyond judgment and analysis, we have the real sense of the view.

Meditation

།དྲི་མེད་སྒོམ་པ་འོད་གསལ་སྙིང་པོ་ནི།
།རྟོགས་པའི་ངང་ནས་བྱིང་རྒོད་སྤྲོས་དང་བྲལ།
།ཡེངས་མེད་བློ་བྲལ་ཡངས་པ་ཆེན་པོ་སྟེ།
།མཁའ་ལྟར་རྣམ་དག་རྒྱ་ཆད་ཕྱོགས་ལྷུང་མེད།
།བསམ་བརྗོད་དམིགས་པ་ཀུན་ལས་འདས་པ་ལགས།

Stainless meditation, the essence of luminous clarity,
Is to be free of dullness, agitation, and proliferation of
thoughts while abiding within the state of knowledge,
An undistracted mind-free great openness
Totally pure like the sky, without any limitation
or partiality,
Beyond all thought, expression, and objectification.

The essence of the practice of Dzogchen is to be in the state of contemplation, which means being in instant presence, our real nature that our teacher introduces us to through direct transmission. When we receive this introduction, we may be able to recognize and remain in our state of instant presence for a few seconds, but then we fall again into our ordinary state of mind, judging and thinking, because this has been our habit for infinite lifetimes. But now we have a kind of example of that state, like having a map and seeing the location of the place we want to go. This example is called son wisdom, and when we are totally beyond any kind of dualistic vision, that is called mother wisdom.[47] Son wisdom is very important for recognizing mother wisdom, because a son always recognizes his mother: even if she is in a large crowd, he will recognize her the instant he sees her. In the same way, if you are a practitioner and have the capacity to be in this son wisdom during your lifetime, you will be able to recognize the mother wisdom when you have died and entered the *bardo* of *dharmata,* the intermediate state of the nature of phenomena.

When you die, all your sense consciousnesses dissolve into your mind and then your mind dissolves into its real nature. At that moment, your primordial potentiality of sound, light, and rays is naked, totally unobscured by dualistic vision. This is the *bardo* of *dharmata,* in which the mother wisdom manifests. If you lived your life as an ordinary person with no knowledge of your real nature, this mother wisdom will still manifest but you will not recognize it, and then your mind will begin to function again and you will wake up as a *bardo* being with a mental body. But if you have the capacity to maintain your state of instant presence at that moment, this son wisdom will recognize its mother wisdom and unite with it, and then you will have total enlightenment in the dimension of *sambhogakaya.* This is not at all uncommon: many Dzogchen practitioners attain enlightenment in this way.

We cannot have realization of the *sambhogakaya* dimension in the *bardo* of *dharmata* without purifying all our accumulations of negative karma, but most of us have infinite negative karma, so even if we have applied methods of purification our whole life long we cannot purify all of it by the time we die. In this case, how is it possible to have total enlightenment instantly in the *bardo* of *dharmata*? It is possible because just being in our real nature is itself the supreme form of purification.

47 See Chögyal Namkhai Norbu, *On Birth, Life, and Death.*

This is something crucially important to understand in the Dzogchen teachings.

In general, the practice of Vajrasattva, with visualization, mantra, and so on, is considered to be the supreme way to purify negative karma, and sometimes people ask me whether they should do this kind of practice to purify themselves, or whether Guruyoga alone is sufficient for this purpose. They have this question because I am always emphasizing the practice of Guruyoga rather than practices like Vajrasattva. Of course, if you have the time and possibility, Vajrasattva practice is also very good, but Guruyoga is really the supreme purification. This is something many people do not understand.

In fact, if we are able to be in our real nature, in the state of Guruyoga, for only a few minutes or even a few seconds, that is millions and millions of times more powerful than Vajrasattva practice. So in this way, when we are in the *bardo* of *dharmata,* just by our son wisdom recognizing its mother wisdom, our infinite potentiality of sound, light, and rays manifests as the peaceful and wrathful *sambhogakaya* deities, and as a consequence all our karma is cancelled and instantly purified.

Even in the Sutra teachings, Buddha said that being in the state of ultimate truth, which is the state of contemplation, even for the time it takes for an ant to walk from the tip of our nose to our forehead, is much better for having realization than if we receive vows and follow them perfectly, do prostrations, pray to Buddha, and make offerings of incense and flowers to him every day for our whole life.

So this is why the state of contemplation, of Guruyoga, is so essential. Even if we do no other kind of practice, Guruyoga alone is sufficient for having total realization. But if this is true, why are we always applying purification methods like the practice of Vajrasattva? Because most people do not have the capacity to be in the state of Guruyoga. So if you have received direct introduction and you do have this capacity, it is very important to make it your main practice and not chase after different methods. Of course, you can use any type of secondary practice that fits your particular circumstances, but you must always remember that the main point is this practice of contemplation, the state of Guruyoga.

Even if you do not discover the state of instant presence when you receive direct transmission from your teacher, you are now connected to the Dzogchen transmission, so you can apply methods for finding that state, and eventually you will discover your instant presence.

Once we have this taste of our state of instant presence, what do we do? We apply different methods to enter into that state again and again, and we try to remain in that state. Then we no longer need to reject any emotions or thoughts by applying antidotes; we do not need to transform them from an impure aspect to a pure aspect. We just remain in instant presence and allow all manifestations of pure or impure vision to self-liberate in that condition.

For example, if I am walking in a garden and see a beautiful flower, as soon as I decide I like it, I also start to want it. Then I feel attachment to that flower, so I decide to pick it. In fact, from the moment I thought, "I like it," I became distracted by the flower. So how should I deal with this? If I am applying the Vajrayana principle, I should transform my impure vision into pure vision to avoid accumulating the ordinary emotion of attachment. I can still think that the flower is nice, I can still enjoy it, but now I have the idea that this flower is something like a flower of wisdom in a pure dimension. Once I have that idea, I can no longer be distracted or accumulate emotions. But if I am a Dzogchen practitioner, I do not care at all whether it is pure vision or impure vision. When I am in the state of instant presence, for me there is no difference at all whether I see a deity or a pig in front of me.

When we explain it this way, some people misunderstand and try to refute the Dzogchen teaching, saying it is dangerous because it does not take the relative condition into account. But this is not true: of course, on the relative level there is a difference between a good thought and a bad thought. But if we are in the state of Dzogchen and a thought arises in our mind, we do not care what kind of thought it is; we do not need to do a kind of Mahayana-style analysis to determine whether it is good or bad. Instead, we self-liberate all thoughts in their real nature.

How do we do this? In the beginning, when we are not very familiar with the practice of Dzogchen, first of all we need to maintain deliberate presence or else we will become distracted and follow after our thoughts. When we have this presence and a thought arises, we notice it and look directly on the face of that thought. This is called *cherdrol*. *Cher* means not just seeing something but looking well. *Drol* means liberation. When we look well at a thought in this way, it self-liberates, so whatever thoughts arise do not create any problems for us; we do not become slaves of our thoughts. Then, as we become more familiar with this process, we no longer have any difficulty remaining present: as soon as a thought arises we have that presence and recognition, and this thought is liberated without our needing to look at it deliberately, as we did before. This is called *shardrol* – liberation upon arising. Finally, when we have become still more familiar, we no longer need any effort to keep from being distracted or to liberate thoughts when they arise: whenever a thought arises, it is liberated in that same moment. This is called *rangdrol* – self-liberation.

When we are in the state of contemplation, we should also be beyond the two conditions of *chingwa* and *göpa*, which are problems we can encounter when we apply meditation. *Chingwa* means our condition is lacking clarity, and if we remain like this we eventually fall asleep.

Göpa means we become agitated, so that even if we want to continue for a little while in our real nature, we suddenly feel the need to move or get up: we want to walk around, we want to do something. But when we are in the state of contemplation, even if these problems manifest sometimes, just by recognizing them and knowing their real nature as they arise, they are also freed in that state.

Our real condition of Dzogchen is like the nature of space: it is pure from the beginning and not subject to any limitations. As we explained before, to discover our real condition, we must first observe ourselves to identify our limitations. Then, when we know we are free from all limitations, there is only the final goal, and we continue in that state.

Conduct

།སྤྱོད་པ་གང་སྣང་བདེན་མེད་དག་པ་སྟེ།
།ནང་གི་འཛིན་པ་གང་ཤར་རང་གྲོལ་དང་།
།ཕྱི་རོལ་གཟུང་བ་རྨི་ལམ་སྒྱུ་མའི་ཚུལ།
།དོན་ལ་གཉིས་མེད་བླང་དོར་མེད་པར་སྤྱོད།

Whatever manifests is unreal and pure:
Inside, whatever grasping concepts arise self-liberate;
Outside, the objects of grasping are like a dream
or a magical display;
In reality, neither of these exist, so the conduct is to act
without accepting or rejecting.

Now we have an explanation of how our attitude or conduct should be. Our understanding of how to apply the correct behavior varies according to the different levels of teachings. But in the Dzogchen teachings, the supreme conduct is to understand that, in the real sense, whatever level of conduct we apply does not exist; it is unreal.

What does this mean for us on a practical level? It means that no matter what our situation, we have the capacity to perfectly integrate with it. We have this capacity because we are not conditioned by anything on the relative level; we do not believe that anything is concrete or important. When we have real knowledge of this, we are free to act in a way that perfectly accords with any situation.

No matter what ideas or thoughts arise in our mind, since we have knowledge of their real nature, they all automatically liberate themselves. And of course, if we are able to be in that knowledge, whenever we have contact with the objects of our senses – all sights, sounds, and so on – these are also liberated, just like a dream or illusion.

What this really means is that we do not need the concepts of something to liberate and someone to do this liberating. We do not need any concept of there being something real that we should accept or reject. Instead, we are always in a state of total integration.

།གཟུང་འཛིན་ཉོན་མོངས་དགག་སྒྲུབ་ཆོས་རྣམས་ལ།
།སྐྱེས་པས་རང་གྲོལ་རང་བཞིན་ཤེས་པས་གྲོལ།
།གྲོལ་བས་ཡེ་རྫོགས་ཆོས་སྐུ་མཉམ་པའི་ངང་།
།འཁོར་བ་སྤངས་ནས་མྱ་ངན་འདས་མི་འཚོལ།

These phenomena – the grasper and the grasped,
emotions, and concepts of negation and affirmation –
Are self-liberated upon arising;
they are liberated by your knowing their nature.
Being liberated, they are the primordially perfect *dharmakaya*
state of equality,
So do not turn away from samsara to seek nirvana.

All the aspects of our usual dualistic vision – subject and object, accepting and rejecting, and so on – self-liberate when we remain in our knowledge of Dzogchen and look them directly in the face. When they are in the state of self-liberation, they are all perfected in their real condition of *dharmakaya*; self-liberation and self-perfection occur in the same moment. If we can practice in this way, everything is simply in its real condition of *dharmakaya*, so we do not need to have the idea, as we do in the Sutra teachings, that we have rejected samsara and now must find nirvana.

།གང་སྣང་དོན་གྱི་གསལ་འདེབས་མེ་ལོང་ལ།
།གང་ཤར་ཤེས་པ་རང་གྲོལ་ཆོས་སྐུའི་རྩལ།
།ཆུ་དང་རླབས་བཞིན་ཆོས་སྐུར་ཕྱམ་གཅིག་གོ
།འདི་ནི་མཐར་ཐུག་དོན་གྱི་དགོངས་པ་སྟེ།
།ལྟ་བའི་ཡང་རྩེ་རྫོགས་པ་ཆེན་པོ་ལགས།

Whatever appears is a mirror showing you
    the real nature,
And whatever arises within it is self-liberated awareness,
    the dynamic energy of *dharmakaya*.
Like water and waves, they are a single evenness
    within the *dharmakaya*.
This is the ultimate and actual state of knowledge,
The summit of all views, Total Perfection.

When we look in a mirror, we know that whatever good or bad appearances manifest are not the real nature of the mirror but only arise through the interdependence of the mirror's potentiality and the object before it. In the same way, our own condition and all our circumstances are manifestations of the energy of *dharmakaya*. So for practitioners, whatever we see, hear, smell – everything we come into contact with through the functioning of our senses – becomes a kind of a secondary cause for self-liberation; everything that manifests makes us recognize its real condition, which is *dharmakaya.* If we are really in this knowledge, then, just like the ocean and its waves, there is no difference for us between *dharmakaya* and all aspects of our impure vision. In that way we liberate everything. This is the final, most important point in the Dzogchen teaching.

།མདོར་ན་གང་ཞིག་ཇི་ལྟར་ཉམས་ལེན་ཀྱང་།
།བདག་འཛིན་རང་གྲོལ་ཉོན་མོངས་དབྱིངས་སུ་དག
།ཐམས་ཅད་ཐབས་ཀྱི་སྤྱོད་ལ་མཁས་པ་ནི།
།ལམ་གྱི་འཁྲུལ་པ་སེལ་ཞེས་བྱ་བར་བསྟན།

In short, whichever of these modes of practice you engage in,
Your ego grasping self-liberates, and your emotions
are purified within the real condition.
Becoming adept at applying these methods to everything
Is what is meant by clearing away illusion on the path.

So now we have a little understanding of the different skillful methods we can apply. But we must remember that the purpose of applying any of these methods is to self-liberate our concept of ego so we can be free from the illusions related to our various negative emotions. This is what we mean by clearing away illusion on the path.

།དེ་ལྟར་ཆོས་ཚུལ་རིན་ཆེན་གྲུ་བོ་ཆེས།
།མ་ལུས་སྐྱེ་རྒྱ་སྲིད་མཚོ་རབ་བརྒལ་ནས།
།ཞི་བ་རིན་ཆེན་ཐར་པའི་གླིང་མཆོག་ཏུ།
།ཟག་མེད་ཞི་བདེའི་དགའ་སྟོན་མཐོང་བར་ཤོག

May the great jewel ship of this way of Dharma
Carry all beings without exception across the ocean
of existence
And lead them to the precious state of peace,
the supreme island of liberation,
To behold the festival of immaculate peace and bliss.

།ཆོས་བཞི་རིན་པོ་ཆེའི་ཕྲེང་བ་ལས།
།ལམ་འཁྲུལ་བ་སེལ་བའི་རབས་ཏེ་གསུམ་པའོ།

From *The Precious Mala of the Four Dharmas,* this is the third teaching, on clearing away illusion on the path.

This precious teaching is like a great ship. By sailing it across the ocean of samsara, all sentient beings can arrive at the real and definitive place of peace, the state of liberation. This is the third Dharma.

The Fourth Dharma:
Purifying Illusion as Wisdom

།དེ་ནས་འཁྲུལ་པ་ཡེ་ཤེས་དག་པ་ཡང་།

Then, illusion is purified as wisdom.

NOW WE COME to the fourth Dharma. Here, Longchenpa explains how the real nature of our karmic vision and our negative emotions is actually wisdom, and how it can manifest in this way, particularly through our application of the teachings of Vajrayana and Dzogchen. So this fourth Dharma is really the essence, the most important part of this teaching.

Provisional Purification

།གནས་སྐབས་མཐར་ཐུག་དོན་གྱི་རིམ་པ་ལས།
།དང་པོ་གནས་སྐབས་ཉམས་ལེན་ལམ་གྱི་དུས།
།ཟབ་མོའི་ཐབས་ཀྱིས་གོམས་པར་བྱས་པ་ལས།
།ཉོན་མོངས་གང་སྐྱེ་དབྱིངས་སུ་རྣམ་པར་དག
།རང་གསལ་ཡེ་ཤེས་མངོན་དུ་གྱུར་པ་ནི།
།འཁྲུལ་རྟོག་ཡེ་ཤེས་དབྱིངས་སུ་དག་ཅེས་བྱ།

> This purification has a provisional stageand a final, definitive stage.
> First, on the provisional stage of the path of practice,
> Having become accustomed to profound skillful methods,
> Whatever emotions arise are completely purified
> in the real condition
> And self-illuminating wisdom manifests directly.
> This is called the purification of illusory concepts
> within the real condition of wisdom.

There is both a provisional way and a definitive way for this to happen. First we have an explanation of the provisional way. Provisional means that we are still on the path, applying different kinds of methods and becoming more and more familiar with them. Through this, our qualities of wisdom manifest in a concrete way; our illusory vision actually manifests as wisdom.

For example, as I explained in connection with the third Dharma, in the practice of Dzogchen, whenever a thought arises, we are not distracted but are present in that moment, and by looking directly on the face of the thought and relaxing in that state of presence, the thought does not give way to more thinking and distraction. In the same way, whatever emotions arise self-liberate and are purified in the nature of wisdom. We discover that our real condition is natural luminosity, and we remain in that state.

།དེ་ཡང་ཐུན་མོང་ཁྱད་པར་བླ་མེད་ལ།
།བསྟེན་པའི་ཐབས་ཀྱིས་སོ་སོར་དབྱེ་བ་ནི།
།གཉེན་པོས་སྦྱངས་དང་ཐབས་ཀྱིས་བསྒྱུར་བ་དང་།
།རང་སར་རྣམ་གྲོལ་མ་སྤངས་དབྱིངས་སུ་དག
།གང་དག་འདོད་ལ་ཇི་ལྟར་བསྟན་ན་ཡང་།
།འགག་པ་ཉོན་མོངས་དག་པའི་དོན་དུ་གཅིག

This can be achieved in reliance upon the methods
Of the common, special, or unexcelled approach:
Respectively, illusion can be cleansed away by means
of antidotes, transformed through special methods,
Or liberated in its own state and purified
in the real condition without being abandoned.
But whichever of these ways you are drawn to
and able to train in,
They are the same in that they bring the emotions
to an end by purifying them.

As we know, we can use the common Sutrayana method to renounce emotions, apply the special method of Vajrayana to transform them, or apply the supreme method of Dzogchen so they can self-liberate in their real condition. But when we attain realization, we are beyond all our problems in the same way, no matter which of these methods we applied.

།འདོད་ཆགས་ཞེ་སྡང་གཏི་མུག་ང་རྒྱལ་དང་།
།ཕྲག་དོག་སྐྱེས་པའི་རང་ས་ངོས་ཟིན་དུས།
།རང་བཞག་རང་གྲོལ་ཡེ་ཤེས་རྣམ་ལྔར་དག
།ཀུན་རྟོག་མེ་ལོང་ཆོས་དབྱིངས་མཉམ་པ་ཉིད།
།བྱ་བ་གྲུབ་པའི་ཡེ་ཤེས་ཆེན་པོ་རུ།
།དུག་ལྔའི་འཁྲུལ་པ་གནས་སྐབས་དག་ཅེས་བྱ།

When you recognize the ground from which attachment,
anger, ignorance, pride, and jealousy all emerge,
By relaxing in your own state [the emotions] self-liberate
and are purified as the five wisdoms.
This is called the provisional purification, in which the
illusions of the five poisons are purified

As the great wisdoms of total discernment, the mirror,
the real condition of phenomena, equality,
and the accomplishment of actions.

Whenever one of our five main emotions arises, we immediately have that recognition and look on the face of that emotion, without trying to abandon it or change it, and by just relaxing in that state our emotions are automatically purified as wisdom. The emotion of anger manifests as the mirror-like wisdom, ignorance manifests as the wisdom of *dharmadhatu* or the real condition of phenomena, and attachment, pride, and jealousy manifest as discriminating wisdom, the wisdom of equality, and the action-accomplishing wisdom. When these five wisdoms manifest in a concrete way in our condition, we consider that we are in the relative or provisional state of purification.

Definitive Purification

།མཐར་ཐུག་ཁམས་ཀྱི་གློ་བུར་དྲི་བྲལ་ཏེ།
།བྱང་ཆུབ་ཞི་བ་རྡུལ་བྲལ་བརྙེས་པ་ན།
།དབྱིངས་ཀྱི་རང་བཞིན་ཅི་འདྲ་མངོན་དུ་གྱུར།
།སྐུ་གསུམ་ཆོས་སྐུ་རོ་གཅིག་ཡེ་ཤེས་བརྙེས།

In the definitive stage, when you are freed from the stains
that temporarily obscured your nature,
And attain the immaculate peace of awakening,
The nature of the real condition manifests directly,
just as it is,
And you attain the wisdom in which the three *kayas*
are of a single taste as *dharmakaya*.

When we obtain the capacity to be fully in our real nature, our condition manifests as the three *kayas* of the fruit. This is the state of the definitive purification. Until we reach this state, our enlightened qualities do not fully manifest, because even though we do have them from the beginning, we also have the provisional, temporary obscurations of dualistic vision, which are like clouds obscuring the view of the sunshine of our primordial state. There is a famous verse in the *Hevajra Tantra*[48] that explains this:

> Sentient beings are themselves buddhas,
> But they are veiled by provisional obscurations.
> When these are cleared away, they are buddhas.[49]

In other words, due to our obscurations, these qualities of enlightenment do not appear to manifest in us now, so we can have no benefit from them. But even if we are in samsara and must deal with many obstacles and negativities every day, our real nature is always pure: it can never be stained by negativities or obstacles, and can never be conditioned by our thoughts and emotions. This is why all our problems in samsara are called provisional obstacles. Realization only means that these obstacles disappear so that all our self-perfected qualities can fully manifest.

This is a very different level of understanding than that found in other kinds of teachings. For example, in the Sutrayana teachings it is considered that we do not have all qualities from the beginning, but instead need to build and develop them. According to the Hinayana

---

48 One of the most important tantras for the Sarma traditions of Tibetan Buddhism, and particularly for the Sakya school.

49 སེམས་ཅན་རྣམས་ནི་སངས་རྒྱས་ཉིད། །འོན་ཀྱང་གློ་བུར་དྲི་མས་བསྒྲིབས། །དེ་ཉིད་བསལ་ན་སངས་རྒྱས་སོ།

system, it is even considered that there are beings called *rigched*. *Rig* means family, and refers to the family of the buddhas; *ched* means that this person is cut off or excluded from that family. In other words, they have no possibility to ever become a fully enlightened being. The Mahayana tradition does not accept this, because it teaches that all sentient beings have the *sugatagarbha*, or seed of buddhahood. For example, a text called the *Uttaratantra Shastra* explains very clearly how the seed or potential of buddhahood is something that all sentient beings possess. This text is very important for the Mahayana tradition, and is considered to have originally been taught by Maitreya.

But, of course, if we have a seed and want a flower, we must first plant that seed in the earth and then make sure that it has water and sunlight, and we must protect it as it slowly develops and becomes a plant that finally produces a flower. So we can see how this idea – that all beings have the potential to manifest the qualities of buddhahood – is very different from our understanding in Dzogchen that all these qualities are already perfected in our condition.

Also, instead of speaking of a seed of buddhahood, the Vajrayana explains that all beings have the condition of the Vajra. But even this refers to a kind of potentiality; it does not mean that our condition from the beginning is the self-perfected state. In fact, the lower tantras' understanding of the potentiality of the Vajra is very similar the Sutra teachings' understanding of the seed of buddhahood. The only difference is that in the Vajrayana it is explained more in terms of the energy level, because the principle of the Vajrayana teachings is always related to the level of energy or speech.

In the higher tantras, we always have the concept of transforming impure vision into pure vision. When we look at a *vajra*, the symbolic representation of the principle of the Vajra, we see that there are five points below, five points above, and a sphere between them in the center.

This sphere in the center represents our real potentiality of the Vajra, and it is this that we should discover through the Vajrayana teachings. How do we do this? By transforming our ordinary impure vision into pure vision. You see, in the symbol of a *vajra,* the five lower points represent the five negative emotions and the upper points represent the five wisdoms, so both our idea of impure vision below and pure vision above are related to the sphere in the center; this is why it is possible for us to transform impure vision into pure vision. So this principle of the Vajra, connected with the concepts of pure and impure, is characteristic of the Vajrayana point of view.

But this too is very different from the point of view in Dzogchen, where we understand that from the beginning everything is the self-perfected state. Another important point of distinction is that in the Dzogchen teachings we say that our three dimensions of *dharmakaya, sambhogakaya,* and *nirmanakaya* have the same flavor, the same condition, which is the *dharmakaya.* This is different from understanding of the three *kayas* in the Sutra teachings, where it is explained that in order to obtain the *dharmakaya* we should practice the Prajnaparamita,[50] which means being in our knowledge of absolute truth, or emptiness. Then, in order to manifest the forms of the *sambhogakaya* and *nirmanakaya,* we should accumulate merit, which means we should apply the other five *paramitas.*[51] These two aspects involve what we call the two accumulations of merit and wisdom. An invocation composed by Nagarjuna for dedicating our merit is a good example of this principle:

50 The transcendent perfection of wisdom.

51 The five *paramitas* related to the accumulation of merit are those of generosity, discipline, patience, diligence, and meditation.

By this virtue, may all beings
Complete the accumulations of merit and wisdom,
And obtain the two sacred *kayas*
Arising from these accumulations of merit and wisdom.[52]

This shows the Sutrayana point of view very clearly. But we must understand that in Dzogchen, and also in the Vajrayana tradition, we say that the *dharmakaya* is never without its qualities, just like the sun is never without its quality of light. For this reason, even if we only practice contemplation, being in our state of instant presence, and do not deliberately try to accumulate merit, we will still have total realization of all three *kayas*. This is our understanding in the Dzogchen teachings.

This actually corresponds to what Buddha said in the sutras – that compared to the merit obtained by someone who makes offerings to the buddhas for his whole life, someone who is in the state of contemplation for just the time it takes an ant to walk from the tip of his nose to his forehead accumulates infinitely more merit.

But of course, this does not mean that we should give no importance to the relative accumulation of merit. Even if we spend our whole day formally sitting in the state of contemplation, we still have to engage in other activities of daily life; at the very least, we need to get up to eat and go to the toilet. And whenever there is movement or activity, whenever we are in the relative condition, we always have the opportunity to accumulate merit. In the relative condition, it is of course much better to do good actions than bad ones. So we should always apply ourselves in this way.

52 །དགེ་བ་འདི་ཡིས་སྐྱེ་བོ་ཀུན། །བསོད་ནམས་ཡེ་ཤེས་ཚོགས་རྫོགས་ཞིང་། །བསོད་ནམས་ཡེ་ཤེས་ལས་བྱུང་བའི། །དམ་པ་སྐུ་གཉིས་ཐོབ་པར་ཤོག

།དག་པ་གཉིས་ལྡན་དབྱིངས་ཀྱི་སྐུ་ཞེས་བྱ།
།རྒྱལ་བ་ཉིད་ལས་གཞན་གྱི་ཡུལ་མིན་པ།
།ཆོས་དང་ལོངས་སྤྱོད་སྤྲུལ་པའི་སྐུ་གསུམ་ཉིད།
།ཡེ་ཤེས་དང་བཅས་ངོ་བོ་ཉིད་སྐུས་བསྡུས།

This is called the *kaya* of the real condition endowed with
twofold purity,
And is the domain of the conquerors alone.
The *dharmakaya, sambhogakaya,* and *nirmanakaya,*
together with their wisdoms,
Are subsumed within the *svabhavikakaya.*

When we no longer have anything obscuring our real nature and have become fully enlightened like Buddha, we have what are called the two purities. First, we have purified all negative emotions, all causes for impure karmic vision, so everything in our dimension manifests in its pure condition. This is called the all-encompassing purity of appearance and existence.

The second kind of purity concerns the qualification of wisdom that allows a buddha to see the karmic condition of all sentient beings and act for their benefit. This is not the same as when sentient beings experience the impure vision of samsara: the cause of that is their own potentiality of karma, whereas buddhas perceive these beings' impure vision through their qualities of wisdom.

So we say that buddhas possess two kinds of omniscient wisdom: the wisdom of quality and the wisdom of quantity.[53] The wisdom of quality means that we know everything as it is according to its real nature. The wisdom of quantity means that even though we no longer

53 Literally "knowledge of the real nature as it is" and "knowledge of the diversity of phenomena."

have any cause for karmic vision, we can see all relative aspects of all sentient beings' karmic vision, all their suffering in the six realms of samsara. Because of this, we can then manifest infinite *sambhogakaya* and *nirmanakaya* forms to work in a way that corresponds to their condition. This condition of the two purities is something we only possess when we become fully enlightened beings like Buddha Shakyamuni. Then we have what is also called the *svabhavikakaya* – the *kaya* of the essence – which means the unification state of the three *kayas* together with their infinite qualities and functions of wisdom.

།རྟག་ཁྱབ་འདུས་མ་བྱས་ཤིང་འཕོ་འགྱུར་མེད།
།ཡིད་བཞིན་ནོར་བུ་ཆོས་སྐུའི་དབྱིངས་ན་བཞུགས།
།དེ་ཉིད་ངང་ལས་ཡེ་ཤེས་ཕྲིན་ལས་སྐུ།
།ལོངས་སྤྱོད་རྫོགས་དང་སྤྲུལ་སྐུའི་རོལ་པ་ནི།
།སར་གནས་རྣམས་དང་འགྲོ་གཞན་སྣང་བ་ཡང་།
།རྒྱལ་བའི་བྱིན་རླབས་གདུལ་བྱའི་བསོད་ནམས་མཐུ།
།ཚོགས་དོན་དག་ལས་དེ་ལྟར་སྣང་བ་ལས།
།སྲིད་པ་ཇི་སྲིད་ཕྲིན་ལས་རྒྱུན་མི་འཆད།
།ནོར་བུ་དཔག་བསམ་ལྗོན་ཤིང་རེ་བ་སྐོང་།
།འདི་ནི་འཁྲུལ་པ་ཡེ་ཤེས་དག་ཅེས་བྱ།

Permanent, all-pervasive, uncompounded, without
transition or change,
This wish-granting jewel abides in the real condition
of *dharmakaya.*
From within that state, by the combined force
of the conquerors' blessings and disciples' merit,
The *kayas* of wisdom activity – the displays of *sambhogakaya*
and *nirmanakaya* –

Appear respectively to those abiding on the *bhumis*
and to ordinary beings,
Manifesting enlightened activity ceaselessly
for as long as samsara remains,
Fulfilling all hopes like a wish-granting jewel
or a wish-granting tree.
This is called the purification of illusion as wisdom.

There is nothing to change in our real nature. It was not created or produced by anybody, and it will remain as it is forever. So we must understand that having realization does not mean that one day something changes for us. We have all the qualities of realization from the beginning; we only need to discover this. That is why it is so important to know the principle of the three *kayas* of the base, the three *kayas* of the path, and the three *kayas* of the fruit; to know that from the beginning the state of all beings is the three *kayas,* and it is only provisional obstacles that prevent us from seeing this.

The *Uttaratantra Shastra* provides an example that is very useful for understanding this. Of course, since it is a Sutrayana teaching, this example was originally intended to help us understand the principle of the seed of buddhahood, not our primordial potentiality. But it applies to this meaning just as well, so it is useful in helping us understand the principle of Dzogchen.

In this story, there was a yogin living on a mountainside, and at the base of the mountain there was also a poor old man living in a cave. Every day, this old man would go to town to beg for food, then return to his cave, eat whatever food he had received, and go to sleep. The yogin would see him go out and return like this every day. But one day he did not see the old man go to town. Several more days passed, and still the yogin did not see the man leave his cave. So with his capacity of clarity, which he had gained through his practice of meditation, he tried to see what had happened, and discovered that the old man had died. Not only this, but he saw that the man had been so poor he did not even have a bed; he just lay on the ground with a stone for a pillow. But then he saw that the stone on which the man had laid his head every night of his life contained a very large diamond within it. All his life, this man had been extremely poor and had really had a miserable life. And every night he would lay his head on this diamond, but because he never discovered it, it was of no benefit to him.

This is just like our situation when we are ignorant of our own self-perfected state. As long as we have not discovered that our real nature is the *dharmakaya,* we will continue to have ordinary, miserable lives in samsara. But when we do discover this and are able to be in this state, it is just as if we have discovered a wish-fulfilling jewel. A wish-fulfilling jewel is something that has an infinite capacity to satisfy all desires: whatever we could possibly want instantly arises from it. So our precious condition of *dharmakaya* is just like that.

From this wish-fulfilling jewel of *dharmakaya,* our potentiality manifests as infinite *sambhogakaya* and *nirmanakaya* forms in order to benefit beings. This is because we have the nondual state of *kadag* and *lhundrub* – our real nature of *dharmakaya* is the condition of *kadag,* or primordial purity, and this condition of *kadag* always has its potentiality of *lhundrub,* its self-perfected qualities.

Sometimes people misunderstand, and think that if they purify themselves of all their karma and attain total realization they will no longer be able to manifest in a human condition, and they do not want this to happen. But as we can see, being in the state of total realization does not mean we lose the ability to manifest in any condition. The difference is that as ordinary beings we are not at all free to choose our situation. Like a small feather in the wind, we are blown around by the force of our karma and can never tell where it will take us. But when we have total realization, we become free: if we want to manifest in some particular part of this world as a particular kind of person or type of being, we can do this. In this way we can be of great benefit to many sentient beings. Only practitioners who already have a high level of realization, like *mahasiddhas*[54] or high level bodhisattvas, can have contact with *sambhogakaya* manifestations. But all ordinary beings can have contact with *nirmanakaya* manifestations and thereby receive the wisdom of enlightened beings.

The Dzogchen teachings explain that all *sambhogakaya* and *nirmanakaya* manifestations arise just like reflections in the mirror of our real *dharmakaya* nature through our primordial potentiality of sound, light, and rays. And like the reflections in a mirror, these forms only manifest in response to secondary causes. In the case of these manifestations, the secondary cause is the relative condition of sentient beings who need our help.

For example, Yamantaka is a wrathful manifestation of Manjushri whose head is similar to that of the class of beings called *yama*. We usually say that Yamantaka has the head of a bull, but this is only an approximation to give us an idea, because humans do not know what a *yama* looks like, and the head of a *yama* is similar to the head of a bull. In any case, why does Yamantaka manifest in this way? Because originally there were some *yamas* who were practitioners with a very high capacity, and they wanted to receive teachings and instructions from Manjushri. Rather than attempting to have contact with him on the *nirmanakaya* or even on the *sambhogakaya* level, they tried to have direct contact with his

---

54 "Great accomplished one." A highly advanced practitioner on the path of Vajrayana.

dharmakaya condition. But of course, since Manjushri's state of *dharmakaya* has no form, it was impossible for them to communicate with him. So, to communicate and teach these beings, he manifested as a *sambhogakaya* buddha in the form of a *yama*, just like a reflection of the form of these beings. Through his manifestation of the *sambhogakaya* form, which is a kind of representative or emissary of the *dharmakaya* state of Manjushri, he was able to communicate with these *yamas*.

All deities whose methods we apply on the Vajrayana path of transformation actually manifested in this way; this is what we mean when we say that the potentiality of *dharmakaya* is just like a mirror. So this is our understanding of the three *kayas* and their functions according to the Dzogchen teachings.

At this point, we must distinguish well between our real nature and its potentiality, otherwise we can have some confusions. For example, when we explain about the three *kayas*, some people misunderstand and think that our real nature is not only the *dharmakaya*, but also the manifestations of *sambhogakaya* and *nirmanakaya*. There is, in fact, one tradition that has this point of view, but it is not Dzogchen. It is called the Jonang school, and it is mainly focused on the practice of Kalachakra. In the *Kalachakra Tantra*, our real nature is called the state possessing all supreme qualities forever, and in general this is understood to correspond to the principle of the Vajra. But the Jonang tradition explains that it means we have the actual manifestation of the three *kayas* forever. This point of view is negated by all the other schools of Tibetan Buddhism, because it does not correspond very much to other teachings, particularly the Sutra teachings. But many people think that Dzogchen teaches something similar to this Jonang view. So we should understand why this is not true.

The Dzogchen teachings speak in great depth about our primordial potentiality, which is self-perfected from the beginning, but there is a great difference between this potentiality itself and that which manifests through it. If we put a mirror in a closed box, it will still have its potentiality to manifest infinite reflections, but it will not manifest anything in that condition because there is no secondary cause. This is how we should understand the difference between our primordial potentiality and the *sambhogakaya* and *nirmanakaya* forms that arise through this potentiality.

But of course, as long as sentient beings exist, the secondary cause for these form *kayas* to manifest is always present, so when we have achieved total realization in the state of *dharmakaya* our potentiality will continually manifest in these ways. This is what becomes possible for us when we transform or self-liberate all our illusions in the state of wisdom.

།དེ་ལྟར་དོན་ཟབ་སྙིང་པོའི་རྟ་བདུན་གྱིས།
།ཡིད་མཁའི་ལམ་ནས་གདུལ་བྱའི་འཛིག་རྟེན་དུ།
།ཚིག་དོན་རྣམ་བཀྲའི་འོད་སྟོང་འཕྲོ་བ་ཡིས།
།འགྲོ་ཀུན་མ་རིག་མུན་པ་སངས་བར་ཤོག

May this seven-horse-drawn sun of the profound
essential meaning
Traverse its path through the sky of the minds
of disciples,
And shine into their world a thousand light rays
of beautiful words and meanings
That cleanse away the darkness of ignorance
from the minds of all beings.

།ཆོས་བཞི་རིན་པོ་ཆེའི་ཕྲེང་བ་ལས།
།འཁྲུལ་པ་ཡེ་ཤེས་སུ་དག་པའི་རབས་ཏེ་བཞི་པའོ།

From *The Precious Mala of the Four Dharmas,* this is the fourth teaching, on the purification of illusion as wisdom.

These teachings are very profound; they are something like the essence of all Dharma teachings. So now Longchenpa makes the aspiration that, just as the sun illuminates the entire sky, the meaning of these words may completely fill the space of our dimension like infinite rays of sunshine, and clear away the darkness of ignorance from the minds of all sentient beings.

This concludes Longchenpa's explanation of the fourth Dharma, on how we liberate our illusions in the state of wisdom.

Concluding Verses

།ཚུལ་འདི་བློ་གྲོས་ཡངས་པའི་ཁང་བཟང་ནས།
།ཐོས་བསམ་སྒོམ་པའི་འབྱོར་པས་རབ་བརྒྱན་པ།
།རང་གཞན་དོན་གཉིས་དགའ་སྟོན་འགྱེད་པ་དེས།
།མདོ་རྒྱུད་མན་ངག་སྙིང་པོའི་དོན་བཞིན་བཀོད།

Within the palace of vast intelligence,
Well ornamented with the riches of listening,
reflection, and meditation,
I have set out this delightful feast of Dharma
that benefits both myself and others
In accord with the essential meaning
of the sutras, tantras, and *upadeshas.*

HERE LONGCHENPA EXPLAINS how he first studied the Dharma, then examined and analyzed what he had learned, and in the end applied his knowledge in meditation. Then, with his wealth of qualities, he wrote down the essence of all the sutras and tantras for the benefit of himself and others.

།དགེ་བ་འདི་ཡིས་བདག་དང་འགྲོ་བ་ཀུན།
།ཚེ་འདིར་སྲིད་པའི་རི་བོ་ཕྱིར་བསྒྱིལ་ནས།
།བྱང་ཆུབ་ཞི་བ་རྟུལ་བྲལ་མཆོག་ཐོབ་སྟེ།
།རང་གཞན་དོན་གཉིས་རྫོགས་པའི་སངས་རྒྱས་ཤོག

By this merit, may I and all beings
Crush the mountain of samsara to the ground
    in this very life,
And attain the supreme immaculate peace
    of awakening,
The total enlightenment that fulfills the aim of self
    and others.

Just as we dedicate our merit at the end of a session of practice, he is dedicating the merit of the writing of this text, and prays that by this merit, he and all sentient beings can overcome samsara and obtain total realization in this life.

།དོན་གསལ་གངས་རི་རྒྱ་ཆེར་མཛེས་པའི་གནས།
།རབ་དཀར་ཡོན་ཏན་ཕྱོགས་ཀྱི་ཐ་གྲུར་ཁྱབ།
།གསུང་རབ་རིན་ཆེན་སྙིང་པོའི་གནས་འཚེར་བས།
།དད་ལྡན་སྐྱེ་བོའི་ཚོགས་རྣམས་དགའ་བར་མཛོད།

The vast and beautiful abode of snow mountains
    of clear meaning
Spreads pure and precious qualities
    to the limits [of space] in all directions.
[Like this,] may the brilliant light of these [four] themes
    of the precious essence of excellent speech
Bring joy to those endowed with faith.

Like a range of snow mountains that are always pure white and shine very brightly, the teachings in this text are very clear, allowing us to clearly see the real meaning of the Dharma. So here we are praying that, with these qualities, this essential teaching can spread throughout our entire dimension and be enjoyed by all people who have interest and devotion.

།ཆོས་བཞི་རིན་པོ་ཆེའི་ཕྲེང་བ་ཞེས་བྱ་བ། །ཐེག་པ་མཆོག་གི་རྣལ་འབྱོར་པ་ཀུན་མཁྱེན་ངག་གི་དབང་པོས་གངས་རི་ཐོད་དཀར་གྱི་མགུལ། མེ་ཏོག་སྤྲིན་གྱི་སྐྱེད་མོས་ཚལ་གྱི་ནང་། ཀུན་ཏུ་བཟང་པོའི་ཁང་བཟང་ཟླ་བ་ཚ་ཤེལ་གྱིས་འཚེར་བར་སྣང་བ་སྟེ་རེ་ཞིག་རྫོགས་སོ། །ཕྱོགས་དུས་ཀུན་ཏུ་བདེ་ཆེན་གྱི་ཆར་བསྐལ་པ་རྫོགས་ལྡན་གྱི་དུས་བཞིན་དུ་འབབ་པས་བསམ་རྒྱུའི་རེ་བ་ཐམས་ཅད་འགྲུབ་པར་གྱུར་ཅིག།

In the excellent house of Samantabhadra, within a pleasure grove of flowers and mist on the slope of White Skull Snow Mountain, this *Precious Mala of the Four Dharmas* was written down all at once, by the shimmering light of the waxing moon, by Kunkhyen Ngaggi Wangpo – Omniscient Lord of Speech – a yogin of the supreme vehicle.
In all places and at all times, may a rain of great bliss descend, just as in the aeon of perfection, bringing all our hopes to fruition.

This explanation of the Four Dharmas of Gampopa was written by the yogin who practices the supreme method of Dzogchen named Kunkhyen Ngaggi Wangpo – one of the many names of Longchenpa – at the place called Kangri Thökar, White Skull Snow Mountain. Kangri Thökar was Longchenpa's retreat place, so it is the most precious and important place associated with him. In general, that area is very dry, but on this mountain top it is always foggy and cloudy, so many flowers grow there.

Then he explains that he wrote this teaching at the time of the waxing moon, in the house of Samantabhadra, which means he wrote it while being in the state of Samantabhadra. If he is in the state of Samantabhadra, his dimension can also be called the house of Samantabhadra.

In the real sense, this is what makes this teaching so important and so precious. In this time of the Kaliyuga, many people follow their own concepts and ideas, reading some books on Buddhism, Hinduism, Taoism, and so on, and then put it all together and invent their own kind of system. They write books about their ideas, and people read them and say, "Oh, this system is wonderful, fantastic! Please hold a workshop!" Then they hold many workshops and become something like a kind of teacher. This situation is only related to our condition of the Kaliyuga; it has no relation to the real transmission of knowledge.

But this text of Longchenpa's is not like that at all; it is not something that Longchenpa invented with his mind. An authentic teaching has a very precise source, a precise transmission, and a precise lineage: what I have explained here is what my teachers taught me and what their teachers taught them, and when we go farther back in this way, we finally arrive at Garab Dorje. When we receive this kind of teaching, we are connected to this lineage and transmission through our teacher. So it is very important to keep this transmission as something like the life essence of the teachings.

How can we perfectly maintain our connection with this transmission? By practicing Guruyoga and being in that state as much as possible, because being in the state of Guruyoga means being in our real nature, and there is no difference between our real nature and the real nature of Garab Dorje and all our teachers. So I hope that all of you will do your best to apply these teachings in your daily lives by practicing Guruyoga as much possible. Then we can have real benefit in our lives, and everything becomes possible.

Bibliography

Bhadantacariya Buddhaghosa. *The Path of Purification: Visuddhimagga.* Translated by Bikkhu Nanamoli. Onalaska: Pariyatti Publishing, 2003

Chandrakirti. *Introduction to the Middle Way: Chandrakirti's Madhyamakavatara with Commentary by Ju Mipham.* Boston: Shambhala, 2005.

Chögyal Namkhai Norbu. *On Birth, Life, and Death.* Translated by Elio Guarisco. Arcidosso: Shang Shung Publications, 2008.

———. *The Crystal and the Way of Light: Sutra, Tantra, and Dzogchen.* Compiled and edited by John Shane. Ithaca: Snow Lion Publications, 1999.

———. *Drung, Deu and Bon: Narrations, Symbolic Languages, and the Bön Tradition in Ancient Tibet.* Translated by Adriano Clemente and Andrew Lukianowicz. Dharamsala: Library of Tibetan Works and Archives, 1995.

———. *Rainbow Body: The Life and Realization of Togden Ugyen Tendzin.* Translated by Adriano Clemente. Arcidosso: Shang Shung Publications, 2010.

———. *The Temple of the Great Contemplation: The Gönpa of Merigar.* Translated by Iacobella Gaetani and Fabian Sanders. Arcidosso: Shang Shung Publications, 2014.

——— (ed.). *The Tibetan Book of the Dead: Awakening Upon Dying.* Translated and annotated by Elio Guarisco. Edited by Nancy Simmons. Arcidosso: Shang Shung Publications, 2012.

———. *Yantra Yoga: The Tibetan Yoga of Movement.* Translated and edited by Adriano Clemente. Ithaca: Snow Lion Publications, 2011.

Gampopa. *dwags po'i chos bzhir grags pa'i gzhung.* TBRC W22712, 1978.

———. *dwag po rin po che'i chos bzhi mdor bsdus pa,* in *gdams ngag mdzod,* vol. 8, ff. 397-400. TBRC W20877. Paro, 1978.

———. *The Jewel Ornament Of Liberation: The Wish-Fulfilling Gem Of The Noble Teachings.* Translated by Khenpo Konchog Gyaltsen Rinpoche. Ithaca: Snow Lion Publications, 1998.

———. *mnyam med dwags po'i chos bzhir grags pa'i gzhung.* TBRC W22712, ff. 1-9. Paro, 1978.

Geshe Sonam Rinchen. *Atisha's Lamp for the Path to Enlightenment.* Translated by Ruth Sonam. Ithaca: Snow Lion Publications, 1997.

Jamgön Kongtrul Lodrö Thaye. *The Treasury of Knowledge, Book One: Myriad Worlds: Buddhist Cosmology in Abhidharma, Kalachakra, and Dzogchen.* Translated by the Kalu Rinpoche Translation Group. Ithaca: Snow Lion Publications, 1995

———. *The Treasury of Knowledge, Books Nine and Ten: Journey and Goal.* Translated by Richard Barron. Ithaca: Snow Lion Publications, 2010.

Longchen Rabjam. *chos bzhi rin po che'i phreng ba,* in *'kun mkhyen klong chen pa dri med 'od zer gyi gsung thor bu,* vol. 1, ff. 247 – 64. TBRC W23555, vol. 2130.

Maitreya, Jamgön Kongtrul Lodrö Thaye, and Khenpo Tsultrim Gyamtso. *Buddha Nature: The Mahayana Uttaratantra Shastra with Commentary.* Translated by Rosemarie Fuchs. Ithaca: Snow Lion Publications, 2000.

———. *Gone Beyond: The Prajnaparamita Sutras, The Ornament of Clear Realization, and Its Commentaries in the Tibetan Kagyu Tradition.* Two volumes. Translated by Karl Brunnholzl. Ithaca: Snow Lion Publications, 2011.

———. *Groundless Paths: The Prajnaparamita Sutras, The Ornament of Clear Realization, and Its Commentaries in the Tibetan Nyingma Tradition.* With commentaries by Paltrul Rinpoche. Translated by Karl Brunnholzl. Ithaca: Snow Lion Publications, 2012.

———. *The Large Sutra on Perfect Wisdom: With the Divisions of the Abhisamayalankara.* Berkeley: University of California Press, 1975.

Patrul Rinpoche. *The Words of My Perfect Teacher: A Complete Translation of a Classic Introduction to Tibetan Buddhism.* Translated by Padmakara Translation Group. New Haven: Yale University Press, 2010.

Sakya Pandita. *rtogs ldan rgyal po'i dris lan,* in *gsung 'bum pe bsdur ma.* TBRC W2DB4570. I: 425 - 431. Beijing: krung go'i bod rig pa dpe skrun khang, 2007.

Shantideva. *The Way of the Bodhisattva.* Revised edition. Padmakara Translation Group. Boston: Shambhala Publications, 2006.

Stewart, Jampa Mackenzie. *The Life of Gampopa.* Ithaca: Snow Lion Publications, 2004.

———. *The Life of Longchenpa: The Omniscient Dharma King of the Vast Expanse.* Ithaca: Snow Lion Publications, 2013.

Index

Buddha Shakyamuni (ཤཱཀྱ་ཐུབ་པ་), 45, 47, 58, 108, 153, 168, 198. *See also* Buddha
Buddha, buddha (སངས་རྒྱས་), 45, 47, 53, 58-59, 67, 72-73, 79, 81-83, 88, 91, 101, 104, 108, 114, 119, 132, 134, 147-148, 153, 161, 166-168, 171, 181-182, 196-198, 202
calm state (གནས་པ་), 56, 104, 160. *See* four yogas
certain assembly (འཁོར་ངེས་པ་), 53
certain place (གནས་ངེས་པ་), 52
certain teacher (སྟོན་པ་ངེས་པ་), 53
certain teaching (ཆོས་ངེས་པ་), 53
certain time (དུས་ངེས་པ་), 53
Chakrasamvara Tantra (འཁོར་ལོ་བདེ་མཆོག་), 160
Changchub Dorje (བྱང་ཆུབ་རྡོ་རྗེ་), 173-174
channels (Skt. *nāḍī*; རྩ་), 27, 157-158
cherdrol (གཅེར་གྲོལ་), 183
chingwa (lack of clarity; བྱིང་བ་), 184
circumstances, capacity, and interest [of the student] (ཁམས་དབང་བསམ་པ་), 166
completion stage (Skt. sampannakrama; རྫོགས་རིམ་), 27, 47, 150, 152, 154, 157-159, 161
concepts, conceptual (རྟོག་པ་), 21, 25, 33, 35, 37, 130, 131, 149, 153-154, 156-157, 162, 179, 184-187, 190, 195, 208
contemplation (Skt. *samādhi*; ཏིང་ངེ་འཛིན་), 11, 13, 45, 96-101, 131, 145, 173, 180-182, 184, 196
craving (ཆགས་པ་), 13, 79, 105. *See also* attachment, desire
cultivation of *bodhichitta* (བྱང་ཆུབ་ཏུ་སེམས་བསྐྱེད་པ་), 130, 138, 141, 143
Dagpo Lhaje (དྭགས་པོ་ལྷ་རྗེ་). *See* Gampopa
dakinis (མཁའ་འགྲོ་), 155
day-long hells (ཉི་ཚེ་བའི་དམྱལ་བ་), 76
desire (འདོད་པ་), 9, 13, 17, 19, 61-62, 85-90, 105, 123-126, 143, 146, 167, 210. *See also* craving
devas (gods; ལྷ་), 5, 7, 58, 66-67, 75, 78-81, 83, 153
development stage (Skt. *utpattikrama*; བསྐྱེད་རིམ་), 27, 47, 150, 152, 154, 156-159

Phonetic Pronunciation Guidelines

An accurate reproduction of Tibetan phonology is not possible using the conventions of any other language, and for readers of Western languages can at most be approached by means of a complex system such as Drajor. Developed by Chögyal Namkhai Norbu, Drajor distinguishes subtle differences in pronunciation using technical devices such as diacritics in addition to the original sounds of letters in Western alphabets. Since the Drajor system is not widely known and requires advance study, Shang Shung Publications adopts a transcription scheme aimed at rendering a pronunciation of Tibetan in a simplified, accessible manner. Still, there are a few points readers should be aware of: while in many respects our system is similar to other common phonetic schemes, such as the one adopted by 84000: Translating the Words of the Buddha and the Hopkins system, we depart from those approaches in an effort to approximate the actual sounds as closely as possible.

For instance, our system reflects how spelling and position change the way a given root letter is pronounced. In some cases, our variances are arbitrary, such as the use of a final *g* rather than a *k*, since in fact the sound is neither precisely a *g* nor a *k*. A *d* after a vowel at the end of a word indicates that the preceding vowel is pronounced (as in Jigmed), in some instances followed by a subtle dental stop (as in *chöd*). Other systems indicate a pronounced final *e* with an *é*, as in Rimé.

The only special characters we use are *ö* and *ü*, specifically when *o* and *u* precede *-d*, *-n*, and *-s* (but not preceding *-l*, and note that *u* preceding *n* is not always umlauted, for example in Kuntuzangmo and *lhundrub*). In English, the easiest way to reproduce the *ö* and *ü* sounds is to keep your lips pursed in the "oo" position and say "er" or "ee," respectively. *Th* represents an aspirated t sound as in the word "tea" rather than th as in "they." The letter rendered as *nga* is a nasalized sound, similar to the ng in "ring." Subscript *r* is retained in our system (*trulku* rather than *tulku*).

All vowels are pronounced as in Italian, regardless whether occurring at the beginning, middle, or end of the word. Thus a is always pronounced as in the English word "attention," not as in "age"; e is pronounced as in the word "best," not as in "she"; i is pronounced as in "in," not as in "island"; o is pronounced as in "origin," not as in "mother"; u is pronounced as in "rune," not as in "butter."

Examples of Voiced/Unvoiced Letters

Letter	Voiced	Unvoiced	Example, Voiced	Example, Unvoiced
ག	g	k	དགེ་ལུགས་ Gelug	གངས་ཅན་ Kangchen
ཇ	j	ch	འཇའ་ལུས་ *jalü*	ཇི་ལྟར་ *chitar*
བ	b	p	སྦས་ཡུལ་ *beyul*	བག་ཆགས་ *pagchag*
ད	d	t	བདག་ *dag*	དག་ *tag*
ཞ	zh	sh	གཞི་ *zhi*	ཞི་ཁྲོ་ Shitro
ཟ	z	s	བཟང་མོ་ *zangmo*	ཟིལ་གནོན་ *silnön*

Some exceptions: Jonang, Bön, *bardo*, Shang Shung